D1617283

EXERCISES

IN

WOOD-WORKING

WITH A SHORT TREATISE ON WOOD

WRITTEN FOR MANUAL TRAINING CLASSES
IN SCHOOLS AND COLLEGES

BY

IVIN SICKELS, M. S., M. D.

Popular Woodworking Books
Cincinnati, Ohio
www.popularwoodworking.com

Distributed in Canada by Fraser Direct
100 Armstrong Avenue
Georgetown, Ontario L7G 5S4
Canada

Distributed in the U.K. and Europe by David & Charles
Brunel House
Newton Abbot
Devon TQ12 4PU
England
Tel: (+44) 1626 323200
Fax: (+44) 1626 323319
E-mail: postmaster@davidandcharles.co.uk

Distributed in Australia by Capricorn Link
P.O. Box 704
Windsor, NSW 2756
Australia

Visit our Web site at www.popularwoodworking.com for information on more resources for woodworkers.

Other fine F+W Media woodworking books are available from your local book-store, or direct from the publisher at www.WoodworkersBookShop.com.

14   13   12   11   10   5   4   3   2   1

A catalog record for this book is available from the Library of Congress at <http://catalog.loc.gov>.

ISBN 13: 978-1-4403-0926-7

media
www.fwmedia.com

PREFACE.

THE exercises in wood-working in this book were prepared by me during the summer of 1883, for the students
of the College of the City of New York. Subsequent
teaching suggested many changes and additions, until the
manuscript was scarcely presentable. This manuscript has
been copied for other schools ; and now, in order that those
who have recently asked for it may receive it in better
shape, this little volume is printed.

I am indebted to Mr. Bashford Dean for the part relat-
ing to injurious insects, which was written expressly for
this book.

I. S.

NEW YORK, *September, 1889.*

CONTENTS.

EXERCISES IN WOOD-WORKING.

INTRODUCTION.

THE tendency of modern systems of education is toward a proper distribution of practical with theoretical training. The mind is to be aided in its development by the action of the eye and hand; and, in fact, all the special senses are employed in objective teaching and manual exercises. In school, the eye does more than interpret the printed page: it recognizes the form and color of objects, it must calculate their size, proportion, and distance, by observing and comparing them; the hand is required to do more than writing: it is taught to appreciate the weight, hardness, and other properties of objects, by actual contact with them. At first the introduction of drawing, modeling, and the use of tools, into the courses of study was experimental; but, having passed beyond that stage, these exercises are now known to be efficient aids to a more natural and rapid as well as stronger mental development.

There are some who, after being educated in the abstract way, can apply their training successfully to practical pursuits, who see no necessity for manual or industrial training in the schools, and who claim that superior and sufficient development may be obtained by the study of mercantile methods and the classics. These, however, form a very small percentage of the people, and systems of education must be arranged to stimulate all intellects, and not measured by the accomplishments of a few. Our best educators recognize this fact, and are modifying old systems by the greater introduction of manual elements. No one doubts the value of practical qualities, not only in ordinary people, but also in prominent leaders, who must be thoroughly practical—a **fact** so aptly illustrated by prosperous manufacturers and merchants, successful engineers, great generals, and eminent statesmen.

Manual training for the early cultivation of these practical qualities in students takes a place in the regular courses of study: by means of it the reasoning power is more easily awakened; knowledge of objects and the facts connected with them are more readily understood and remembered; and, above all, the accuracy and precision demanded by the practical studies, lead to closer observation and exactness in others. This training begins in the lowest grades, and continues in its various applications through all the classes, until in the higher grades we find sufficient physical strength to handle the ordinary wood-working tools.

The prime object of all manual training, especially in this country, is to aid mental development, and while this fact must not be lost sight of, the training should be in some useful art, or in some exercises which are introductory to the useful arts.

Perhaps the most valuable of these studies is industrial drawing, which is in itself a sort of universal language, a medium between thought and execution. Its study cultivates precision, and is well calculated to develop sound and accurate ideas. Drawing naturally precedes construction, it prepares the way for the work of the engineer, manufacturer, or builder. Even the ideas of the inventor are jotted down in a chance sketch, which is added to and modified at leisure, leading to the finished sketch, from which the skilled draughtsman produces the designs for the execution of the work.

The studies of drawing and wood-working are closely connected, and may be taught together with great advantage to both. A simple object is roughly sketched on paper, its measurements accurately made and marked on the sketch; from this a drawing is made with instruments, either full size or to a scale, which is used in the workshop as a guide to the construction of the object. Skill in sketching is a valuable acquirement, and should be taught early in the course of industrial drawing. These sketches should, if possible, be made from real objects, instead of charts, and should always be accompanied by measurements. In sketching it is well, first, to determine the number of diagrams necessary to show the form or structure of the object, and allot for each a certain space on the paper; second, to place each sketch in the middle of its space, of which it should occupy about one half, thus leaving a margin for notes, measurements, and small details; third, to draw the relative proportions of the object as accurately as possible; fourth, to mark on the sketch the measurements of each part.

Wood-working from the simple constructions of earliest times has advanced with the necessities and customs of nations, until at present it includes the complicated structures of modern requirements. Throughout all wood-working trades we find certain general principles regarding the cutting action of tools on wood, and the joining of different pieces; and, since those principles are more easily taught by carpentry and joinery, these branches have been generally adopted as educational aids.

The very extensive use of wood for building has given rise in this country to a craft of carpenters whose improved tools and methods of work are superior in many respects to those of European workmen. Based upon these methods, workshop practice in schools and colleges as applied to woodwork does not stop with carpentry: its design is to prepare the way for the entire field of mechanical arts; so that carpentry and joinery are followed by turnery, carving, and possibly a few lessons in pattern-making. These should be followed by metal-work, such as forging, chipping, filing, and, finally, with the elements of machine-work. The study of mechanics as thus taught in the educational workshop should be applied correctly, by methods which are the actual but intelligent practice of the operating mechanic. As to the time required, it can not be expected that the three to five hours per week spent in the workshop are going to make mechanics; far from it: several years of labor and experience are necessary to produce skilled workmen in any of the arts.

This book deals with carpentry and joinery, and is divided into two parts:

The First Part treats of the structure, properties, and kinds of wood; its manufactures and economic relations to other substances, parasitic plants and insects; and means of preserving wood.

The Second Part contains the exercises, preceded by a description of tools, and the manner of drawing used to illustrate the exercises.

These exercises are based upon American methods of work and have been taught as follows: Each exercise was explained, illustrated by sketches on the blackboard, and then executed by the students. As the exercises advanced, the blackboard sketches were prepared with more detail, each being shown with its measurements designated. The students copied these sketches and noted down such of the verbal directions as they could. With the higher exercises it was found necessary to issue duplicate copies, describing and illustrating each step in construction, and also to exemplify by models made by the instructor.

Exercises 1 to 8 introduce the chief wood-working tools and methods of marking. These exercises should be executed with much care and patience, and if necessary repeated, to insure better results in subsequent work.

Following exercise 8 are directions for sharpening tools. But students should not attempt to sharpen tools until they have had considerable practice in the use of them; especially saw-filing, which requires remarkably good judgment, keen eye-sight, and a steady hand.

Exercises 9 to 20 give instructions for marking out and shaping simple joints.

Exercises 21 to 27 instruct in the methods employed in uniting several pieces to make a complete structure.

Exercises 28 to 35 give the details of ordinary house-carpentry, from which the student may obtain particulars for the construction of models, and the apprentice the actual building of the various parts making up a wooden dwelling.

Exercise 36 shows the use of the frame-saw, and methods of bending wood.

Exercise 37 gives an example of pattern-work, and illustrates the manner of uniting pieces for economy of labor.

Exercise 38 instructs in shaping by the use of templets.

Exercise 39 treats of veneering, followed by directions for painting and polishing.

PART FIRST.

STRUCTURE OF WOOD.

IF we examine the stem of a young plant, we find three distinct tissues composing it: On the outside is the bark or protecting tissue (a, Fig. 3) ; inside there is a soft material, made up of many-sided, thin-walled cells, which constitute the living portion (b, Fig. 3) ; and arranged in a circle in this soft tissue are several fibrous bundles (c, Fig. 3), giving to the stem its strength to support the branches and leaves. Because of differences in the character of these bundles, we separate stems into three classes; and the pine, palm, and oak may be taken as types of each.

In the pine and oak the bundles are similarly arranged, and consist of an outer portion called **bast** (d, Fig. 3), and an inner portion called **wood** (e, Fig. 3) ; between these is a thin layer of active cells, which multiply by division to form the bast and wood; this layer is called **cambium** (f, Fig. 3), and adds each year to the size of the bundle. In the palm the bundles arise from active cells at the growing point of the stem, and continue down the stem, sometimes becoming smaller, but retaining a rounded form.

As the stems grow older and larger, we find, in the pine, that new and branching bundles appear between the first ones, forming, during the season, a circle of bundles, which constitutes the first **annual ring**. This ring is interrupted by plates of tissue communicating between the pith, on the inside of the ring, and the soft tissue on the outside. In a cross-section of the stem these plates are seen as lines, called **medullary rays,** radiating from the center toward the bark. At the

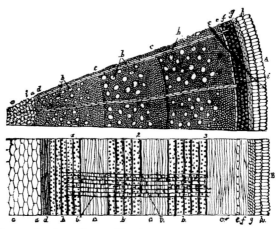

Fig. 1.—Diagram of a stem with a cambium layer. A, section cut across the bundles ; B, section in the direction of the bundles ; 1, 2, 3, first, second. and third annual rings ; *a, a,* pith ; *b, b,* pitted vessels ; *c, c,* wood-cells ; *d,* spiral vessels, found only in the first annual ring ; *e,* cambium-cells ; *f, g, h,* layers of bark ; *i, i,* medullary ray. (After Carpenter.)

end of the season growth stops, to be resumed again in the spring. The slow and condensed growth of summer, and the rapid, open growth of spring, give rise to a peculiar mark in the bundles which indicates each year's increase, so that by counting these marks or the annual rings we may ascertain the age of a tree.

The last few rings formed are engaged in transporting or storing up nourishment, and give rise to what is called the **sap-wood.** The rings inside of the sap-wood serve only for support, and make up the **heart-wood** of the tree.

In the palm, new bundles arise, placed irregularly in the soft tissue or **pith,** and by tracing these bundles throughout the plant we see that they extend, usually without branching, from the apex of the leaf to the small ends of the roots, so that for each new leaf there will be in the stem new bundles.

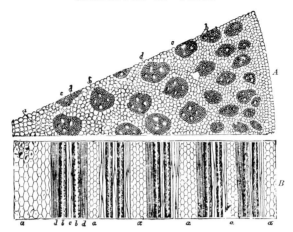

Fig. 2.—Diagram of a palm-stem. *A*, cross-section ; *B*, longitudinal section ; *a, a.* soft tissue ; *b, b*, vessels or tubes with pitted sides : *c, c*, wood-cells or fibers ; *d, d*, vessels with spiral markings. (After Carpenter.)

In the oak we have the same appearance regarding the annual rings and medullary rays as in the pine :

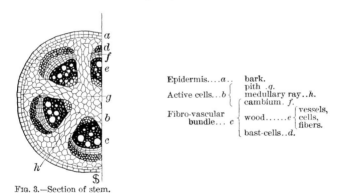

Epidermis....*a* . .	bark.
Active cells...*b*	pith .*g.*
	medullary ray..*h.*
	cambium. *f.*
Fibro-vascular bundle... *c*	wood......*e* { vessels, cells, fibers.
	bast-cells..*d.*

Fig. 3.—Section of stem.

Examining more closely these wood-forming bundles, we find them composed of cells with a variety of forms and walls of varying thickness and peculiar markings. In the pine group the cells are long, with pointed ends, and walls marked by characteristic elevations called **bordered pits** (Fig. 4). These pits arise during the thickening of the cell-wall, which can not take place on the thin circular membranes (Fig. 10, *c*), through which the sap passes, but forms arches with open tops over them, and thus gives the bordered appearance. In

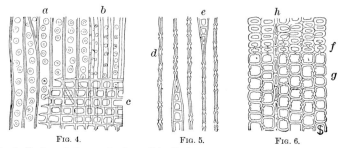

Fig. 4.   Fig. 5.   Fig. 6.

Fig. 4.—Section of pine-wood cut parallel with the medullary plates. *a*, spring growth, with large bordered pits ; *b*, summer growth, with smaller bordered pits ; *c*, medullary tissue.

Fig. 5.—Section at right angles with the medullary plates. *d*, bordered pits ; *e*, medullary tissue.

Fig. 6.—Cross-section of the same. *f*, summer growth ; *g*, spring growth ; *h*, medullary ray.

the heart-wood these thin membranes have broken down, allowing a free passage of air or water through the cells. In spaces between the wood-cells there are, in most of the pines, canals containing resin dissolved in turpentine. The thin plates of tissue forming the medullary rays are composed of small cells, with thin walls in the outer annual rings, but in the heart-wood with walls very much thickened.

The isolated bundles of the palm are composed of various elements, some of which simply support, as the bast and wood fibers ; others support and conduct, as the vessels and wood-cells ; these latter convey air, and water charged with mineral matters absorbed by the roots.

The bast-fibers are on the outside, surrounding the bundle, and are very long, narrow, many-sided cells, with pointed ends, the walls very much thickened and marked with oblique pores. The wood-fibers are on the inside of the bundle, similar to the bast-cells in every respect, except that they are shorter, and occasionally used for conducting and storing up nourishment. The vessels or tubes are large and few, and present varied markings; the larger are pitted, the smaller either

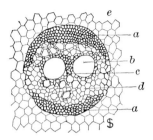

FIG. 7.—Palm-bundle. *a, a,* bast; *b,* pitted vessel; *c,* wood-cells; *d,* smaller vessels; *e,* soft tissue.

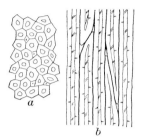

FIG. 8.—Bast-fibers.

ringed, spiral, netted, or ladder-form. The wood-cells are like those of the pine group, but with simple in place of bordered pits. There are present, also, sieve-tubes with clusters of small perforations in sides and ends, and a group of long, thin-walled cells similar to the cambium-cells of the pine and oak. Frequently in the vicinity of the vessels are found thin-walled cells with blunt ends, separated from the vessels and surrounding cells by membranous pores; these cells, which are somewhat similar to cambium-cells, serve the purpose of conducting and storing up the organic materials formed in the leaves.

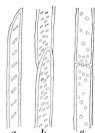

FIG. 9.—Pitted vessels.

In the oak group the wood is composed of compact bundles made up of the same fibers, cells, and vessels found in the palm, with the exception of the bast-fibers, which are formed outside of the cambium zone and constitute the inner bark. In the spring growth the vessels are large and numerous; in the autumn they are much smaller, and in some cases may be absent. By this variation in the size and position of the bundles the annual rings become distinctly marked. The medullary rays in the heart-wood vary in thickness, and in many of the woods the cells composing them become solid.

2

COMPOSITION OF WOOD.

Newly formed cells have the wall composed of **cellulose, a** substance similar to starch in composition. The contents of the cell are made up of a number of substances, the chief of which are albuminoids, starchy matters, oils, and water with dissolved sugars, gums, and acids.

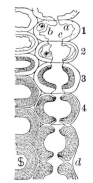

FIG. 10.—Diagram showing growth of the cell-wall.

1. Cambium-cell : *a*, protoplasm or living contents of the cell ; *b*, nucleus in the protoplasm ; *c*, thin membrane through which the sap passes. In the heart-wood this membrane has broken down, as at *d*.
2. Protoplasm forming a wall of cellulose.
3. Protoplasm has disappeared. Cellulose changing into lignin.
4. Cell-wall composed of lignin and thin membrane.

In the heart-wood the contents have disappeared, air taking their place, and the cell-wall has become very much thickened by a deposit within the cellulose of a dense substance called **lignin**, which gives to wood its elasticity and hardness.

In the living tree, air and water are present in varying quantities, depending on the season and kind of wood. The amount of water is frequently as much as fifty per cent. During the seasoning of pine, about twenty per cent of water is removed from the wood. This may be called **free water**, because it exists in the plant with all the ordinary properties of water. But there is also in pine-wood about the same amount of water, which is chemically combined with carbon to form cellulose and lignin. The presence of this **modified water** may be demonstrated by placing the wood in a partially closed iron vessel, and heating it red hot; the wood is reduced to charcoal, while water is given off, together with a small quantity of gases, oils, and other matters.

The elementary composition of wood varies according to the kind, the soluble matters in the soil, and the amount of moisture absorbed by the tree. Generally wood contains large quantities in proportion of carbon, hydrogen, and oxygen; less of nitrogen, sulphur, and potassium; and small quantities of iron, phosphorus, calcium, sodium, and silicon, with traces of many other elements.

If wood is burned in the open air, the carbon, hydrogen, nitrogen, sulphur, and part of the oxygen are driven off in gaseous form; the other elements remain, and constitute the **ash**, of which the principal ingredient is potassium.

The amount of ash is greater in the palms and least in the pines. The percentage of a few are as follows:

Oregon pine	0·08	White oak	0·41
Red cedar	0·13	Hickory	0·73
Redwood	0·14	Black walnut	0·79
Chestnut	0·18	Palmetto	7·66
White pine	0·19	Black iron-wood	8·31
Whitewood	0·23	Spanish-bayonet	8·94

BRANCHING OF STEMS.

In the middle of a forest, trees grow straight, tall, and slender, as in Fig. 12, because it is necessary for them to

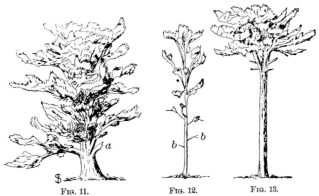

FIG. 11.   FIG. 12.   FIG. 13.

FIG. 11.—Shape of a tree on the border of a forest. *a*, broken branch exposing surfaces for boring insects or fungus spores.
FIG. 12.—Young forest tree. *b, b,* branches die for want of sunlight.
FIG. 13.—Shape of forest tree with straight stem and crown of small branches and leaves.

push up the tops in order that they may receive sufficient sunlight, to enable the leaves to digest the plant-food and increase the diameter and height of the stem. Lower branches last only a few years, then die, and are broken off (*b*, Fig. 12). On the margins of the forest and in open places, trees send out numerous branches, and stems become large in diameter, but remain short (Fig. 11). The bordering trees, while they serve as a protection from the wind for those inside, furnish knotty and cross-grained lumber; those inside produce the straight-grained and valuable wood (Fig. 13). Members of the palm group rarely have branching stems. In growth, the stems remain long and slender, but frequently larger at the top than at the base.

AGE OF TREES.

Like animals, in growth and development plants are subject to influences of climate and nourishment. In its proper latitude, and with an abundance of water and food in the soil, a tree adds to its annual growth and lives to a great age. But when the soil becomes exhausted of the necessary elements, or a more robust species crowds roots and leaves, then a tree begins to show signs of decay. It is difficult to establish rules regarding the proper age for cutting. For timber, most trees are considered fit at about one hundred years, although oak may furnish excellent timber at two hundred years. The purpose for which the wood is to be cut determines the proper age. Young trees show a closer grain and give a more elastic wood than old ones. Very old trees, although apparently sound, are found to be partially decayed in the middle of the trunk, so that the elasticity and hardness of the wood are replaced by a characteristic brittleness.

DECAY OF TREES.

As long as a tree is in a healthy condition, its top or crown retains its small branches, but when these refuse to send forth leaves, and break off, it is a sign of decay, and the tree should be cut down and put to some use; for, if allowed to stand, its decay, aided by parasitic insects, will proceed rapidly until there remains nothing but a shell, composed of the growing zone and a few of the last annual rings, and its value for any purpose will become very much lessened or entirely lost.

Breaking or sawing off a branch and leaving the wound exposed will furnish an opportunity for fungus spores or boring insects to begin the destruction of the wood.

Cutting down trees on the border of a forest, or clearing a large space within it, is destructive to the tall trees remaining exposed to the winds and elements. The swaying of the stems in a storm causes the tender root-hairs to be broken off, thus preventing absorption of sufficient nourishment by the root, and shortening the life of the tree.

The proper time of the year for cutting down trees is an important matter. In the spring and late summer the outer portion of the wood is charged with elements which tend to hasten its decay. In the drier summer months and in winter the growing and conducting cells are less active or altogether dormant, and better wood may be secured if cut during those times of the year. Oak is said to be more durable if cut just after the leaves have fallen.

The trees are cut with axe or saw, and skill is required to fell a tree so that it will come safely to the ground, and not hang suspended to neighboring branches or crush young trees in its fall. An experienced woodman will direct the falling tree exactly where he wishes. He cuts on the side and about at a right angle to the direction in which he wishes the tree to fall; next he cuts on the opposite side, and, if necessary, a few inches higher.

The tree, after falling, is cleared of its branches and sawed into lengths, according to the future use of the wood.

MILLING.

If near a stream, the logs are rolled or drawn to the water and floated to the mill, where they are examined and grouped according to fitness for special uses. A long immersion of the logs in water removes soluble substances in the sap-wood, but is said to injure the heart-wood by rendering it less elastic. Water, however, is the easiest and cheapest means of transporting logs. In the absence of an available stream, the logs are carried on wagons or sleds to a railway or directly to the mill.

The old-time mill, with its single upright saw and ancient water-wheel, is seldom seen nowadays; it has given way to gang and circular saws, and even to giant band-saws, run by turbine or steam. Frequently portable engines and saws are employed on the ground where the trees are cut, thus saving the transportation of the waste portions of the logs.

Logs are sawed into either **timber, planks,** or **boards,** and these constitute **lumber.** Timber includes all of the largest sizes, such as beams and joists. Planks are wide, of varying lengths, and over one inch in thickness. Boards are one inch or less in thickness, and of varying lengths and widths. Lumber may be **resawed** into the many smaller sizes which are to be found in the seasoning and storing yards.

The rough-sawed lumber may be planed at a mill, and is then called **dressed** lumber, of which there is a great variety, adapted to almost every purpose for which wood is used. Dressed planks and boards when free of all defects are called **clear**, and their regular sizes are $\frac{5}{8}$, $\frac{7}{8}$, $1\frac{1}{8}$, $1\frac{3}{8}$, and $1\frac{1}{8}$ inches, which are one eighth of an inch less in thickness than sawed lumber. One-half-inch dressed is made by resawing one-and-a-quarter-inch lumber.

DRYING OF WOOD.

In the preparation of lumber for use, it is necessary to remove its moisture, after which the wood is **seasoned.** The planks and boards after sawing are placed in large square piles in the open air, each layer separated by three or four narrow strips or boards laid in the opposite direction. By this means a free circulation of air takes place throughout the pile; the drying is gradual and thorough, if allowed sufficient time. For ordinary carpentry, two years is considered enough, but for joinery at least four years should be allotted to the seasoning. Many processes have been devised to hasten the evaporation—such as kiln-drying, in which the wood is placed in chambers heated by steam or hot air, or by the employment of vacuum-pumps together with heat. All are inferior, however, to the open-air seasoning, in that they cause a rapid drying of the surface and ends, with a slow or imperfect drying of the interior; thus impairing both the strength and elasticity of the wood.

It is difficult to give rules for testing wood to determine whether it has been properly seasoned or not. One way is to push a knife-blade into the wood, and note how much it sticks when withdrawn. Another is to cut a shaving from the board, and note its elasticity, brittleness, or strength. Experienced workmen crush shavings in their hands to determine the character of the wood.

As the wood loses its water it shrinks perceptibly, much more in the direction of the annual rings than in the direction of the medullary rays, and very little, if at all, in the direction of the fibers. If we examine the end of a log which has been exposed to the weather, we will find cracks extending from the center toward the circumference, and which penetrate from a few inches to a foot or more into the log (Fig. 14). These cracks, called **wind-checks**, are seen in planks and boards, and cause the ends to become waste wood. To prevent this rapid drying, the ends of the logs are tarred or painted. If the lumber is piled soon

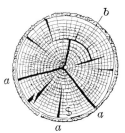

Fig. 14.—End of oak-log exposed to the weather. *a*, wind-check; *b*, shake.

after sawing, these wind-checks are smaller, and the waste portion is consequently less.

WARPING.

Because of the unequal shrinking of the wood in drying, the planks and boards have a natural tendency to **warp** or curl. Those cut farthest from the center of the log warp the most, while those at the center remain nearly flat. Lumber seasoned under pressure, such as that exerted in the pile in the open air, dries straight and true; but, if it should be resawed into boards of half the thickness, it will require further seasoning to avoid warping. This tendency to warp is sometimes

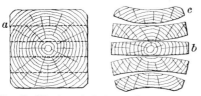

seen in very old wood; for instance, in planing down an old mahogany table - top to remove scratches, what was perfectly straight and flat before now warps and twists to a remarkable degree. This shows the

FIG. 15.—Warping of planks cut from an unseasoned log.

necessity of using, in construction, lumber of the same thickness in which it has been seasoned.

Another cause which changes the shape of wood is its tendency to absorb moisture, either from the air or the ground. This makes it necessary to protect exposed surfaces with paint or varnish. Pieces of work, in process of construction, should stand endwise and not lie on the floor, even if it seems perfectly dry. Lumber in the workshop is kept in racks hanging from the ceiling. These racks are so arranged as to allow the boards to rest on one edge, and to be separated by vertical strips. In this manner the boards are easily accessible, and the seasoning process is continued by the warmth of the room.

Properties of Wood.

Grain.—We have seen that wood is composed of long, hollow wood cells, or fibers, sometimes accompanied by vessels of varying diameters. The character and direction of these fibers constitute what is termed the **grain** of the wood. As these fibers separate and break more easily lengthwise than across, we say that wood splits with the grain. If the fibers run very straight, the wood is **straight-grained**; if crooked, then it is called **cross-grained**. Many causes affect the regularity of the grain: the stem itself may be crooked, it may be straight, but the fibers run spirally around it, or there may be sets of fibers alternating in spiral directions; branches and wounds also cause cross-grain.

If the cells are small and compact, the grain is said to be

fine, as in box-wood ; if nearly uniform in size and thickness, the wood is **even-grained,** as in maple. The cells may vary greatly in size and thickness, and have large vessels in the spring growth, which would give rise to **coarse-grained** wood, as in the oak, ash, and chestnut.

The appearance given by the annual rings and medullary rays to the surface of the wood differs very much with the kind of wood and the part of the log from which the board is sawed. Special cuts are made to obtain the best effect of these markings. To show **silver-grain,** the face of the board should be parallel, or nearly so, with the medullary rays. The birch is an excellent example of this effect. Maple and ash are frequently seen with a wavy or **curled grain.** For veneers, which are about one sixteenth of an inch in thickness, wood with a very irregular grain is selected, such as walnut roots and knots, and knurls of mahogany. In some old maple-trees an appearance called **bird's-eye,** due to a small circular inflection of the fibers, gives to the wood a fine effect.

Woods in which the grain runs alternately in different directions, though hard to split and very difficult to work and finish, usually furnish an ornamented grain, such as mahogany.

Density.—This property depends on the more or less complete thickening of the walls of the wood-cells, and also upon the number and size of the vessels. Certain operations, such as turning, carving, and wood-engraving require dense or close-grained woods.

Porosity.—A porous wood has large, thin-walled cells and many open vessels. Its open grain is easily filled with preserving liquids which adapts it for framing and timber work generally ; if such a wood is to be finished, the pores must be filled before a good surface can be obtained. As a rule, porous woods are soft and light, while dense woods are hard and heavy.

Weight and Hardness.—It sometimes happens that the entire cell is replaced by the thickened cell-wall, and this, together with deposits of oily and resinous substances, make an exceedingly hard and heavy wood. On the contrary, we have very light woods, even lighter than cork; these are composed of thin-walled cells filled with air. Between these extremes are found many gradations of weight and hardness, but woods are generally spoken of as hard or soft, and heavy or light. The hard and heavy woods are stronger and more durable than the softer and lighter ones.

The weight is expressed by a number, which shows the weight of the wood compared with the weight of an equal bulk of water, taken as the standard.

During the process of drying, wood becomes lighter and harder; thus, lignum-vitæ and most of the palms are quite soft and easily cut when green, but after drying are worked with great difficulty.

Strength.—The strength of wood depends on peculiar powers of resisting various forces brought to bear upon it. Thus, lignum-vitæ and the oaks are noted for their **stiffness**, or resistance to bending, which is probably due to the interlacing of their fibers. Young hickory, lance-wood, and others are very **elastic**, bending readily and returning to their former position without injury to the structure. Black or swamp ash and young white oak split easily into long and strong strips or bands such as those used for making chair-seats or baskets. Very little force is required to break the fibers of whitewood, birch, and mahogany across the grain. Pine, ash, and maple break easily but with a splintered fracture. In some palms this splintering occurs to such a degree, that walking-sticks may be transformed into very dangerous weapons, which has given rise to laws in some countries restricting their use. Rattan, oak, and hickory, when bent short, have the individual fibers unbroken, but separated from each other; and are therefore **tough** woods. Hard and dense woods resist compression, while soft woods yield to pressure and are indented; and more so when the pressure is applied on the sides than on the ends of the fibers. This **compressibility** of the softer woods is taken advantage of in gluing up joints, where the pieces are forced into perfect contact by the pressure of the screws. To secure a good joint with hard woods it is necessary to use the greatest care in preparing and cutting the pieces. The cohesion of the particles of the fibers, when strains are applied lengthwise, is very great, several tons being required to fracture pine one inch square.

Color.—As the heart-wood becomes lignified, coloring-matters are deposited within the substance of the cell-wall, giving to each kind its characteristic colors; these are exhibited in great variety, including every shade of color between the white of satin-wood and the black of ebony. In the same wood there may be variations of tint, or even color, in the annual rings and medullary rays, enhancing the beauty of its appearance. The sap-wood receives none of the color-pigments, and therefore is always light or even white. As a rule, exposed surfaces, whether varnished or not, become darker; and this darkening, besides indicating age, gives to the surface a more agreeable effect than that of new wood. It is for this reason, as well as deception, that new cabinet-work of hard wood is stained to imitate the effects of age. Color combined with a figured grain constitutes the intrinsic ornament of wood.

Durability.—At great age a slow oxidation of the constituents of the cell-wall takes place in the interior of the heart-wood of standing trees, thus rendering the wood softer and brittle, and an easy prey to the fungi and insects. Dampness, by promoting fungus growths, is very destructive to cut timber, few woods withstanding its injurious influence; especially is this so when there are alternating dampness and dryness as seen in those portions of a building or structure in contact with the soil. Most woods if kept dry and protected from insects with paint or varnish, will last for ages, as illustrated by ancient pieces of furniture. Nearly all woods are perfectly preserved if kept immersed in water, which is shown by the wood of vessels that have been sunk for a hundred years or more, and which finds application in laying the foundations of stone for large buildings and bridges upon the tops of piles driven below the water-mark. Many woods like cedar and camphor-wood have within their substance oils and resins which protect them from the fungi and insect life.

DEFECTS IN WOOD.

Some of the defects found in lumber, as wind-checks, cross-grain, warping, and improper seasoning, have already been alluded to. Wood may be **shaky** (*b*, Fig. 14), which is a separation of the annual rings, showing checks or splits, sometimes including nearly all of the central portion and extending throughout the length of the stem. No wood furnishes a better example of this than hemlock. This shaky condition is caused by the swaying from the force of wind, acting upon trees in open places, along the borders of forests, and especially those adjoining cleared tracts.

Knots in the wood are imperfections arising from the deflection of the fibers which form branches. Near the center of the stem the fibers are few and the knot small, but as the stem enlarges in size the number of fibers in the branch increases so that at the circumference of the stem the knots are largest. The great strength required at the union of

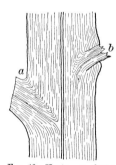

branch and stem is shown by the superior hardness and density of the wood composing the knot. Dead branches give rise to **loose** and dark-colored knots (Fig. 16, *b*), and the fibers of the stem that form afterward bend around the branch, continue up the stem, and produce cross-grained wood in the vicinity of the knot. **Fast** knots are the result of living branches, and boards containing them may be used wherever strength or finish is not required.

FIG. 16.—Knots. *a*, fast ; *b*, loose.

Sap-wood.—The edges of boards frequently retain a portion of the sap-wood, which must not be placed in any permanent structure, because of its softness and tendency to induce decay.

Resin-pockets are spaces between the annual rings of pine timber, filled completely or in part with resin. These slightly weaken the board, and if used in any portion of a building exposed to the warmth of the sun, will exude drops of turpentine, even if the surface has been painted or varnished.

Decay.—Of all the defects in wood, decay or rot is at once the most prevalent and disastrous to the strength and usefulness of the material, and, when begun, will continue until the whole of the wood is consumed.

Defects in milling are frequent. Lumber may be uneven in width or thickness. The saw may have torn out fibers in places, or have cut irregularly, so that, in planing the boards, marks of the saw remain. When the edges of boards are not squared, they are termed **wany.**

Measure and Value of Wood.

Timber and lumber one inch or more in thickness are sold by the **square foot**, meaning one foot square by one inch thick, or containing one hundred and forty-four cubic inches. Boards less than one inch in thickness, and veneers, are sold by the square foot, face measure. Lumber which is finished at the mills for special purposes may be sold by the **running foot**, or length in feet, as moldings; or by the **piece**, as fence-boards, studs, and many kinds cut to standard sizes. A few are sold in quantity, as fence-pickets, laths, or a **bundle** of shingles, intended to cover a certain area. Many of the more expensive and fancy woods, such as lignum-vitæ and box-wood, are sold by the pound.

Values of wood vary with supply and demand as well as with quality and appearance. Durability and a figured grain are especially sought for. Fashion also, in dictating the material as well as the style, determines the demand for the hard woods, particularly those used for furniture and the interior wood-work of houses. Thus we find a succession of favorites, each of which, after serving a few years of preferment, has been set aside to make room for the next. Beginning with mahogany and rose-wood, we note black walnut, ash, ebony and its imitations, and again mahogany, as having been the choice, until at the present day, oak, neglected for many years, is the leading wood.

Kinds of Wood.

In this list are given the woods commonly used by carpenters and joiners, together with their chief characteristics.

Pine Group.

White Pine, commonly called **pine**, is a rapidly growing tree in the Northern United States and in Canada. It attains a large size in favorable soils, and furnishes a light, soft, not strong wood, with a close and straight grain. The annual rings are marked by narrow summer growths, and the medullary rays are very fine and numerous. The color is a faint yellowish brown, darkening with exposure. Its abundance, the ease with which it is worked, and its power to hold glue, make its use very extensive, especially in all carpentry-work where an easily finished wood is desired. It is one of the best woods for making patterns for casting.

Georgia Pine, of the South Atlantic and Gulf States, is a large forest tree with smaller annual rings than pine, and with a broad, dense, resinous, and dark-colored summer growth, which gives to the wood a well-marked grain. In radial section the numerous and fine medullary rays are scarcely visible. The wood is heavy, hard, strong, and durable, becoming harder and somewhat brittle with age. It is used for heavy timbers, floors, and, because of its grain, sometimes as a trimming wood.

The many other species of pine have local or limited use. Among them the yellow or Jersey pine is perhaps the best known, as it is largely manufactured into lumber. Its properties are about intermediate between white and Georgia pine

Black Spruce grows in about the same regions as white pine, and furnishes a wood very similar to it, excepting that it is more resinous. This and white spruce are commonly called **spruce**, and are used extensively for inferior work.

Hemlock.—A species similar to spruce, grows in the Northern States. Its wood, which splits or breaks easily, is light, moderately soft, has a coarse, uneven grain, and is frequently shaky. It holds a nail much better than pine, which fits it for rougher building material.

White Cedar.—Abundant in the Atlantic States, supplying a soft, light, fine-grained, and durable wood, suited for a variety of purposes where durability rather than strength is required. The annual growth is of moderate size, made up of very small wood-cells, traversed by exceedingly fine and numerous medullary rays. It is used in boat - building, cabinet - work, cooperage, cigar - boxes, and shingles.

Red Cedar is a small tree of slow growth, widely distributed in various soils, usually rocky, but reaching its largest size in swamps. The wood is like white cedar, but more compact, even-grained, and durable. It is reddish-brown in color and extensively used in cabinet-work, because of its strong odor, which repels insects. Its durability makes it valuable for posts, sills, and other structures in contact with or near the ground.

Cypress.—This tree of the Southern swamps grows to a great size. It furnishes a most valuable wood, because of its durability, which is claimed to be superior to that of all other woods. It is light brown in color, and in structure similar to white cedar, with larger wood-cells. Its timber is preferable to pine in trimming brick houses, and in all parts exposed to the weather. In the South its employment is as general as that of pine in the North.

Redwood.—Of late years the wood of the giant fir-trees of California has been introduced into the chief lumber markets of the country. The wood-cells are large, the compact summer growth constituting about one quarter of the annual increase. The color is a dull red, the quality very durable, while the wood shrinks perceptibly in the direction of the grain. In other respects this wood resembles pine, and is used for general construction as well as ornamentation.

Palm Group.

While in many tropical countries the palms supply the inhabitants with many necessities, as building-woods, starch, sugar, fruits, fibers for ropes and cloth ; in temperate climates the abundance of better material limits the use of the palm group.

Palms.—The numerous kinds differ in height, diameter, and structure. The fibro-vascular bundles vary in size and number, are exceedingly hard, and the surrounding pith either soft or very hard and solid at the outside and soft with few bundles on the inside. Usually the wood cuts easily when green, but only with the greatest difficulty when dry. Besides the use of the **palmetto** for wharf-piles, some of the palms are combined in cabinet-work, and used for canes and handles.

Rattan.—A long, slender, trailing palm, furnishing a tough, flexible material, which enters largely into the manufacture of furniture,

Bamboo.—A gigantic member of the grass family, grows in the tropical regions of America and Asia, and has a limited use in cabinet-work. Its hollow, jointed stem adapts it to many inferior uses, such as canes and handles, and when split and joined in a peculiar way forms the much-prized fishing-rods.

Oak Group.

Birch.—Among the many species of birch, the cherry or black birch supplies the best lumber. The wood is heavy and strong, colored brownish-red, with a fine, compact, and evenly marked grain, due to the absence of many vessels in the annual rings, and has very small but visible medullary rays. It is used in ship-building, turning, and extensively in cheap furniture.

White Oak is the standard by which the strength, durability, hardness, and other qualities of the various woods are compared. It is distributed generally throughout the eastern half of the United States, grows to a large size, and furnishes superior timber. Large vessels in the spring growth occupy from one third to one half of the narrow annual rings. The medullary rays are large, thick, and exceedingly hard. The wood is heavy, hard, strong, difficult to split radially, coarse-grained, and colored a light brown. It is used in structures requiring great strength, and especially in ship-building, cooperage, and carriage-making.

Red Oak.—A very large forest tree of the United States. It furnishes a heavy, hard, and strong wood, with a very coarse grain, due to a large number of vessels of uniform size crowded into the first half of the annual growth, and also to the large and thick medullary rays. The wood is reddish brown, durable, and used extensively for furniture and cabinet-work generally.

Chestnut.—A very large forest tree common in the Atlantic States, having a characteristic coarse-grained wood. The annual growth is considerable, frequently over half an inch, in which the vessels are numerous, large in the spring wood, but gradually becoming smaller toward the summer growth. The medullary rays are small and indistinct. The wood is light, moderately soft, breaks and splits easily, is remarkably durable exposed to the weather and not in contact with the soil. The tree reaches its best condition at about fifty years of age, after which it is very liable to decay in the middle of the heart-wood. It is well adapted for the coarser parts of a building, is used to a small extent in cabinet-work, and extensively for out-of-door structures.

Beech.—A large forest tree growing generally east of the Mississippi, provides a heavy, hard, and strong wood. It has a fine, even grain, is of a light color, and has large medullary rays. It is used to a limited extent for furniture, but more for implements, especially plane-stocks.

Black Walnut is one of our finest and largest timber-trees, growing in the central and eastern portions of the United States. It furnishes long, wide planks and boards of superior qualities. The wood is moderately heavy and hard, dark, porous, and marked by a beautiful grain. It is strong, durable, and not liable to the attacks of insects. The annual rings contain many vessels, and the medullary rays are ex-

3

ceedingly small. At one time it was the favorite wood, and
extensively used for internal decoration and fancy-work.
It is still largely used combined with veneers from roots and
knurls of European varieties. Gun-stocks are almost exclusively made of walnut.

Butternut is a small species of walnut, giving a light and
soft wood, with a well-marked grain. Its lumber is short in
length, not liable to split, noted for its resistance to heat and
moisture, and the ease with which it receives paint or polish.
It is used in cabinet-work.

Hickory is a tree of branching habit, found commonly in
the United States. Its wood is heavy, tough, very strong, and
usually cut into planks. The annual rings are indistinct
and crowded with fine vessels, or marked by a narrow zone
of larger vessels. The medullary rays are very broad, numerous, and distinct. The flexibility and toughness of the
wood cause it to be extensively used in the construction of
implements, tools, carriages, etc. Difficulty of working and
liability to the attacks of boring insects prevent its use in
building.

Buttonwood, or sycamore, is the largest tree of the oak
group in the United States. It furnishes a heavy, hard, light-
brown wood, with a fine, close grain. It is readily polished,
easily broken, and difficult to work. Throughout its annual rings are small vessels, very numerous in the spring
growth. The medullary rays are numerous and thick, and
give to the radial section a silver grain similar to that of
beech but more strongly marked. The great liability of the
wood to decay, and its tendency to warp, restrict its use to
structures thoroughly protected from the atmosphere and
moisture.

Ash.—A large tree growing in the colder portions of the
United States, furnishes a moderately heavy, hard, strong,
and very elastic wood. The annual rings are compact, with
large vessels in the spring growth. The medullary rays are
numerous, small, and thin. The wood is coarse-grained,
light brown, and extensively used for implements and machinery, for furniture and cabinet-work. Its liability to

decay, and its brittleness with age, prevent its use in heavy work.

Apple.—The reddish-colored wood of the familiar fruit tree, is moderately heavy and hard, has a very compact and fine grain. The annual rings are narrow with small vessels, and the medullary rays are very fine and crowded. The wood is preferred for tool-handles, turnery, and smoking-pipes.

Pear.—In structure the wood of the pear-tree is similar to that of the apple. It becomes hard and dense when dry, and yields readily to edge tools. Its almost grainless character adapts it for a variety of purposes, particularly carving and the coarsest kinds of wood-engraving.

Wild Cherry.—A tree common in the United States, furnishes a moderately heavy, hard, and durable wood. The annual rings are wide and evenly filled with small vessels. The medullary rays are fine, crowded, and light red in color. The grain is fine and close, and the wood easily polished. It is brownish red in color, and used extensively for cabinetwork. After several years the wood becomes very brittle.

Locust.—One of the largest forest trees, growing generally throughout the United States. Its hard, yellowish wood is composed of very wide annual layers, in which there are comparatively few and large vessels arranged in rows. The medullary rays are well marked and numerous. Although it polishes readily, it is used only to a small extent in cabinetwork, but finds a demand in exposed structures, where great durability is necessary, as in ship-building, supports for buildings, posts, etc. Its hardness, which increases after manufacture, makes it a favorite with turners.

Sugar-Maple is a timber-tree of large size, growing in the northern parts of the United States and in Canada, which, besides furnishing a sap rich in sugar, gives a light-colored, fine-grained, hard, strong, and heavy wood. Its annual growth is narrow, with small vessels scattered through it. The medullary rays are small and distinct, giving to the radial surface a well-marked silver grain. In the older trees, wavy or curled grain, or the inflection called bird's-eye, may appear, enhancing the beauty and increasing the value of the wood. Were it not for its want of durability, its hardness and handsome, silky grain would make it our most valuable wood. It is used for a great variety of purposes—building, implements, machine-frames, work-benches, furniture, fancy-work, and turnery. Curled and bird's-eye maples are frequently sawed into veneers.

Mahogany.—A native tree of the West Indies and Central America. It is a very large and most valuable tree, furnishing a durable and handsomely marked wood. Its color varies from yellowish to reddish brown; its hardness from a moderately to an exceedingly hard wood; and its grain from straight to the most crooked contortions. The annual rings are large, and contain a few large, scattered vessels. The medullary rays are very fine and crowded. A peculiarity in the growth of mahogany is the alternating obliquity of the fibers of one annual layer to those adjoining; this is sometimes over ninety degrees between fibers four or five layers apart. The straight-grained varieties have little tendency to warp, but the cross-grained ones warp and twist to a remarkable degree. The wood is used for many purposes—machine-frames, work-benches, all kinds of furniture, cabinet-work, interior finish of dwellings, and patterns.

Lignum-vitæ.—A West India wood, exceedingly heavy and hard. The annual rings are almost solid, containing a few small and scattered vessels. The medullary rays are very numerous, but difficult to make out. The wood is very resinous, hard to split because of the obliquity of the fibers of the annual layers, and dark brown in color; it is soapy to the touch; is used for small tools, bowls, and in turnery; and is well adapted for block-pulleys.

Basswood is a large tree growing generally throughout the Northern United States and Canada. It furnishes a light, soft wood, with the general appearance of pine. The annual layers are filled with very small vessels, the medullary rays numerous and distinctly seen in radial sections. Though not strong, the wood is difficult to split, and has a great tendency to warp. It may be easily bent, thus adapting it to a variety of uses, especially the curved panels of carriages and sleighs.

Whitewood is the wood of the tulip-tree, a large, straight-stemmed forest tree, growing in most of the United States. The wood. is light, soft, breaks easily without splintering, does not split with the grain when dry, shrinks excessively in drying, and is very liable to warp and twist. The annual rings are very large, with numerous small vessels throughout, giving a fine grain. The medullary rays are very numerous and distinct. The cheapness, ease with which it is worked, and large size of its boards, cause the wood to be used in carpentry and cabinet-work in many places where pine is better suited.

Rosewood.—The wood of several foreign trees growing in Brazil, Canary Islands, Siam, and other places. The annual rings are narrow, almost solid with resinous materials, and with a few very large, scattered vessels. The medullary rays are very fine but perceptible on the smoothed surface. The wood is heavy, hard, brittle, takes a high polish, and has a characteristic odor and taste. The grain is remarkably handsome, those kinds with alternating dark-brown and red markings being most prized. Besides tool-handles few things are made of the solid wood; it is sawed into veneers which are extensively used in cabinet-work.

Boxwood.—A tree growing in Southern Europe and Asia, furnishes a heavy, hard wood with a peculiarly even, almost structureless grain. The annual rings are very narrow, with many small, scattered vessels. The medullary rays are very fine and numerous. Boxwood is yellowish in color, and is used for many purposes—in turning, model-making, and particularly in wood-engraving, in which it has no equal.

Ebony.—A dark, sometimes jet-black wood, from several foreign countries, the best coming from the Mauritius. The wood is heavy, hard, very strong, with an almost solid annual growth, in which there are very few open vessels. The medullary rays are very fine, but visible. It has an astringent taste, takes a high polish, and is used for many small articles, in turnery, and in cabinet-work.

Table of Woods, with their Chief Qualities compared by Simple Numbers.

COMMON NAME.	Scientific name.	Weight. Water = 1·00.	Hard-ness.	Bend-ing.	Break-ing.
White Pine.....	*Pinus strobus*	·39	1	5	3
Georgia Pine ...	*P. palustris*	·70	4	10	9
Black Spruce ...	*Picea nigra*	·46	1	7	4
Hemlock	*Tsuga Canadensis*	·42	2	5	4
White Cedar....	*Chamæcyparis sphæroidea..*	·33	1	1	1
Red Cedar......	*Juniperus Virginiana*......	·49	4	3	4
Cypress	*Taxodium distichum*.......	·45	2	6	3
Redwood	*Sequoia sempervirens*	·42	1	3	3
Birch	*Betula lenta*...............	·76	7	9	9
White Oak	*Quercus alba*	·75	7	6	6
Red Oak	*Q. rubra*	·65	5	7	7
Chestnut	*Castanea vulgaris*	·45	2	5	4
Beech	*Fagus ferruginea*..........	·69	6	8	9
Black Walnut...	*Juglans nigra*	·61	6	7	5
Butternut	*J. cinerea*	·41	2	4	3
Hickory	*Carya alba*...............	·84	9	9‑	9
Buttonwood	*Platanus occidentalis*	·57	5	5	3
Ash............	*Fraxinus Americana*	·65	5	6	5
Wild Cherry....	*Prunus serotina*	·58	6	5	5
Locust	*Robinia Pseudacacia*	·73	8	8	10
Sugar-Maple....	*Acer macrophyllum*	·49	5	4	4
Mahogany......	*Swietenia mahogani*	·73	10	6	7
Lignum-vitæ....	*Guaiacum sanctum*	1·14	(28)	5	5
Basswood.......	*Tilia Americana*	·45	1	5	2
Whitewood	*Liriodendron tulipifera*	·42	2	5	3

WOOD AND IRON.

Before the great advancement in the manipulation of iron and steel, wood had a much more extended application than exists at the present day. Structures such as buildings, furniture, and implements, were made entirely of wood; the pieces were stiffened by wooden braces and the joints fastened by wooden pins. But the superior strength of metal, and the convenience which attends its use in connection with wood, have led to great changes in the manner of construction and the form of the work. Wooden pins and hand-made nails have given way to machine-cut nails and screws, and the superior joints obtained by the latter allow the wooden parts to be made of different kinds and much lighter than before.

In America, where wood is plentiful and cheap, dwellings

and buildings generally are made of this material. In portions of the larger cities where the houses are necessarily high and crowded, the danger attending the use of such a readily inflammable substance as wood has led to the adoption of brick and stone for the walls, and metal or slate for the roofs.

Lightness of weight and the natural beauty of its grain will always insure the employment of wood in the manufacture of furniture, and for the trim and interior decoration of houses. To secure lightness and elasticity in implements and machinery, many parts must be constructed of wood.

Temporary structures, such as scaffolding and the false work of bridges and trestles, are built of wood, and require almost as much care in their construction as if intended to be permanent.

In ship-building, iron and steel have almost supplanted the employment of wood. Their superior strength and firmness at the joints make safer and faster vessels.

As a direct result of the progress in the manufacture of iron and steel, most of the wood-working tools and machinery have been greatly modified and improved. This is best seen among the measuring, boring, and planing tools, which have so changed that greater accuracy, easier work, and better finish are now within the power of every workman. Among the machines may be found appliances for imitating many of the operations formerly done by hand, and, while this may seem to be an encroachment upon the province of the workman, it must be remembered that the proper care and adjustment of these machines, and the accurate union of the pieces shaped by them, necessitate a thorough knowledge of the manipulation of the hand tools.

WOOD-WORKING TRADES.

While one or two men in a small community may furnish all the wood and metal work needed by it, in large towns and cities the great amount and variety of work required necessitate a division of labor, resulting in numerous trades or crafts. Some of these are exclusively wood-working, others metal - working, while a few combine portions of both.

To follow or employ any one of the trades intelligently and successfully, the underlying principles governing the use of all sharp tools must first be thoroughly understood and acquired by practice. Upon this knowledge as a basis the numerous details of forms and joints, of arrangement and adaptation of different materials, must then be accumulated by years of work and study to produce a mechanic in any one of the various pursuits.

Carpentry.—Of all the wood-working trades carpentry is the most general. It includes the cutting and framing of large timbers and rough planks and boards for building houses, bridges, trestles, piers, ship-frames, and the like. The form, size, and arrangement of the timbers necessary to resist the strains are designed by an engineer or architect, but the details, and especially those of the joints, must be determined and laid out by the carpenter. The woods made use of in carpentry are usually pine, hemlock, spruce, oak, and chestnut. The tools employed are the larger hand-saws, ax, adz, strong chisels, brace and large bits, hammer, and mallet; and for marking, a chalk-line, tape measure, large steel square, and carpenter's pencil, together with plumb-line or level; as a general thing, these complete the outfit.

Joinery differs from carpentry in that the work is smaller and made smoother; and the form, size, and joints established by experience and long usage are constructed to give a finished appearance as well as strength. All the commoner and fancy woods, together with bone, ivory, and some of the metals, are used in the many branches of joinery. The tools, besides those of the carpenter, include the finer saws, chisels, and gouges, the various forms of planes, smaller boring-tools, and measuring-tools, such as try-squares, bevels, gauges, compasses, and finely divided rules.

As necessary adjuncts to joinery we have turnery and carving, with modified forms of chisels and gouges for ornamental work; and painting for finishing and preserving work.

Some of the applications of joinery create distinct trades, such as cabinet and furniture making; stair, sash, and door making; pattern and model making; carriage and boat building, and cooperage—all of which require special woods and modified forms of tools adapted to the particular and various forms and joints peculiar to each.

In America there are many mechanics well versed in both carpentry and joinery of ordinary house-building, and who are known by the general name of carpenter.

PARASITIC PLANTS.

The forms of plant-life destructive to living trees and lumber belong to the higher orders of the group **Fungi**. These are parasites—that is, they do not possess chlorophyl (the green matter common to the higher orders of plants), and therefore do not assimilate or digest food for themselves, but live on the digested and structural material of others. They are developed from minute **spores,** grow and decay very rapidly, and contain a large amount of nitrogen in their composition.

The structure of these fungi consists of two portions—a tangle of thread-like filaments having somewhat the appearance of the root-hairs in the higher orders of plants, and which have for their function the absorbing of nutritive material for the fungus; and a denser portion composed of straight filaments, which form on their extremities the spore-bearing cells.

In developing, the fungus starts from the spore, which corresponds to the seed of the higher orders. This spore sends out a long filamentous tube which, as it progresses, gives off branches, and these in their turn branch until the tangle of filaments. called the **mycelium** is formed. This my-celium may have long and separated filaments, as in the underground portion of mushrooms, or it may have the filaments massed together, as seen in some polyporous fungi under the bark of trees. When the mycelium has absorbed sufficient nourishment to produce spores, it sends out the straight branches usually into the light. The mycelium is about the same in all the different fungi; the variations in the form and color of the spore-bearing portion, and the characteristics of the spores, giving to each kind its place in classification.

The exact conditions which cause the spore to develop a mycelium are not known, but it may be generally stated that it must find a resting-place containing nutritive elements peculiarly suited for its growth, and, as accompanying conditions, warmth, moisture, ammonia, and an absence of strong light.

Some of the fungi obtain their food from the contents of the living cells of the plant, so that the mycelium destroys by entering and depleting the sap-wood of the tree. In others the mycelium secretes a peculiar juice, which has the power of decomposing the lignin of the heart-wood, and converting it back into cellulose, which is dissolved and absorbed by the fungus. The latter destroys by removing those elements which give to wood its strength, and causes a condition in the tree or lumber known as **decay** or **rot**.

In the heart-wood the vessels and cells facilitate the growth of the fungus in the direction of the grain, while its progress across the grain is comparatively slow. In passing to adjoining cells the filaments of the mycelium may go through the pores, or by the solvent action of its secretion make openings for itself.

Fig. 17.—Mycelium of fungus piercing wood-cells. *a*, filaments; *b*, holes formed by fungus.

The extent to which these fungi will grow depends on the supply of food material, so that, once established in the stem of a tree, they may spread until the entire structure is consumed. If their filaments pass through the soil, like those of some of the toadstools, many trees may be affected and destroyed by one fungus. The innumerable mass of spores given off by the fungus would seem to predict the entire destruction of timber-trees, but fortunately this is prevented by the difficulty of satisfying the peculiar requirements necessary for the development of the spores.

Among the parasitic fungi those which are especially destructive to wood belong to the group HYMENOMYCETES, or those having naked spores growing on exposed surfaces. In the agarics, or toadstools, these surfaces are thin, flat plates, called gills. In the polypores, or tree-fungi, the spore surfaces are tubes whose openings constitute the pores. In *Merulius,* or tear-fungus, the spore surfaces are shallow cavities.

The toadstool (*Agaricus melleus*) is very destructive to many trees, including the firs, pines, beech, and oak. Its mycelium consists of long, dark filaments several inches below the surface of the ground, that gain access to the wood by attacking the roots and sending its filaments up into the stem. The spore-bearing portion is frequently seen in the autumn at the base of dead trees; it is yellowish, and has the gills extending partly down the stem, on which is a well-marked ring. Besides scattering its spores, the danger from this fungus consists in its power to send filaments through the soil from one tree to another.

FIG. 18. — Toadstool. *a,* stem; *b,* umbrella top; *c,* ring, attached to the top before it expands; *d,* gills; *e,* filaments forming the mycelium.

The tree-fungus (*Polyporus annosus*) is very destructive to the pines and firs. Its mycelium is white, silky, and forces its way through the bark of the roots into the living cells, and from them into the heart-wood. The spore-bearing portion may appear on the lower part of the trunk or upon the roots underground. The porous surface is turned upward and the spores transported by insects or burrowing animals from root to root. The *Polyporus sulphurus* is one of the best known of the destructive fungi, and attacks almost every kind of tree. Its mycelium develops from spores which lodge in the stump of broken or sawed branches, and passes downward into the stem consuming the tissue as it goes. Its sporing portion is bright yellow on the under or porous side and red above, usually

projecting from the decayed stump of the branch or in advanced cases from the side of the stem.

P. pini is similar to the *P. sulphurus,*
and is a **wound-parasite** on the pines.

P. fulvus is also a pine-tree fungus, peculiar in its action, in that it does not dis-
solve the lignified parts of the cell, but the
thin membranous substance which unites
the cells, thus setting the cells free. *P.
dryadeus* acts in a similar way in oak-trees.

Fig. 19. — Polypore
growing on a living
locust-tree.

Merulius lacrymans affects pine and
spruce timber in houses, and especially the
ends of joists and beams in contact with
damp brick or stone walls. Its mycelium penetrates the
end wood, causing **dry rot** and forms on the surface of the
wood and adjacent brick-work a flat, moist mass which develops on its under side shallow spore cavities. All fungi
contain large quantities of water, but the *lacrymans* frequently holds an excess which exudes in small drops from
its spore surface.

The *Dædalia* is closely related to the *Polyporus,* and is
parasitic on white cedar and cypress.

Among the higher forms of fungi the *Dematium gigan-
teum* is very destructive to oak; noted cases of its ravages
being the destruction of oak piles along the sides of the Canal
du Midi, Toulouse, and the destruction of the Foudroyant, a
sixty-gun vessel, in two or three years.

The moist condition of standing timber adapts it to the
attacks of the fungus mycelium. In cut timber, warmth and
moisture, with bad ventilation and imperfect seasoning, all
favor the growth of the fungus. An examination of the
wood, as the mycelium progresses, shows at first a darkening,
usually of a brown tint, due to the action of the fungus secretion on the wood. Then the wood becomes yellowish, with
black spots surrounded by white masses of cellulose, derived
from the decomposed lignin of the cell-walls. This cellulose
is slowly absorbed by the mycelium, the wood assumes a
light-brown color, and is very soft and brittle. When the

thin membrane which unites the cells becomes dissolved, then the wood loses its form and breaks down into a brown powder, leaving a hollow trunk.

TIMBER-BORERS.

From the outer bark to the innermost heart-wood, all trees have enemies, more numerous if not more destructive than man. If we go to the nearest saw-mill or wood-pile, almost the first thing we notice is the worm-eaten appearance that so many timbers present. If, now, we stop and examine one of these logs with a little care, we may make out the directions of the borings, and probably find the cause of these depredations in the form of a small, white-bodied grub. A little further study of the various woods in the neighborhood will show us:

1. That borings in the same log may be made by different kinds of grubs.

2. That special kinds of borers infest certain kinds and conditions of woods.

3. That the softer parts of the tree, such as sap-wood or wood in decay, are far more frequently infested than the harder parts.

4. That, on account of the more porous structure, the grub is apt to follow the grain of the timber, rather than pass through a number of more compact rings of growth.

We have thus far been considering the case of wood in the green state, but we may find that these principles of borers may be applied as well to seasoned woods, save that this class is not usually attacked until decay has commenced. Any method of softening the wood, as heat, cold, or moisture, aids its destruction by insects. The destruction of timbers under water such as wharf or bridge piers, or ship-bottoms, is hardly a part of the present theme. It may be noted, however, that what the insect does on land, the mollusk, boring sponge, and marine worm accomplish in salt water; and that such destruction is apt to be most rapid near the low-water mark.

Thus far we have seen where the borings occur; let us now consider the insect itself, and its method of work.

Probably all the borings we have so far seen have been the work of beetle-grubs. We must remember that beetles, like butterflies, and like nearly every other insect, must pass through a series of changes or transformations before they become what we regard as beetles. The egg laid by the adult beetle on the proper food-supply hatches into a minute **grub**. This grub, or **larva**, sets at once to feeding, grows continually, and sheds or molts its outgrown skins until it

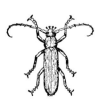 

Fig. 20.—Oak-pruner.   Fig. 21.—Its larva.   Fig. 22.—Its pupa.

attains a limit of size. Thence the insect passes into a curious, mummy-like **pupa** stage; and it is from this dormant state of transition that the beetle finally emerges. Keeping in mind this life-history, we may see how from the egg in some crevice of bark the grub has steadily eaten its way inward to its proper food-supply, whether in sap-wood or heartwood, and has there grown and prospered. As the period of this feeding life in many borers extends over years, we may understand how much damage is apt to be done. The grub spends its time feeding and resting, frequently retracing its way to the outer opening, and enlarging its gallery whenever necessary. A large amount of the waste sawdust, sometimes freshly cut, sometimes glued into pellets by the insect's secretions, is continually being pushed out of the boring and allowed to drop to the ground, whitening the bark of the tree and readily revealing the insect's whereabout. When about to transform into the pupa the grub usually fills up the outer opening with chippings, stuck together, in order to conceal itself from enemies, especially from the sharp-eyed woodpecker. Sometimes, instead of this method of protection, the insect will inclose itself in a strongly made cocoon of chippings; but in either case the glue-like matrix is readily dissolved by a secretion of the escaping insect.

The way in which the grub is enabled to bore into the hardest woods is certainly of singular interest, and gives another example of the wonderful muscular development of the insect, more wonderful than the leg-muscles of the grasshopper or even than the wing-muscles of the humming-bird moth. If we take any common beetle, whether perfect or in the grub stage, and examine for a moment the mouth parts, we may readily make out a pair of short, thick jaws, or **mandibles**, moving sidewise, reminding us of the tinsmith's shears, protected by flap-like lips, one in front and one behind. It may be seen, from the way the lips are hinged at their bases, that they may serve to hold the object to be cut, and that they are aided in this by a pair of small, jointed appendages inserted near the under lip. The mandibles themselves, if more closely examined, will be seen, like the shears, to press their cutting edges together as they meet side by side, but we must note that the cutting edges are short and curved, somewhat like the edge of a gouge. The pivot on which the jaws rotate is located at the extreme outer margin of the mouth, and the heavy muscles which start from the back of the insect's head are attached solidly to the movable jaw between the pivot and curved, or gouge-like cutting edge, so as to gain an immense leverage. The boring is in reality a process of countersinking, the insect frequently changing from a right to left motion, to one from left to right, and it is by some believed that in this change the jaws are sharpened. As a rule it may be stated that the jaw of a hardwood borer has a short, strong, cutting edge, and that the particles of wood cut are exceedingly minute. So nicely are the cutting powers adjusted that instances are recorded of the boring of sheet-iron by an escaping beetle. A Central American wood-beetle (*Zopherus*), kept alive this winter in a

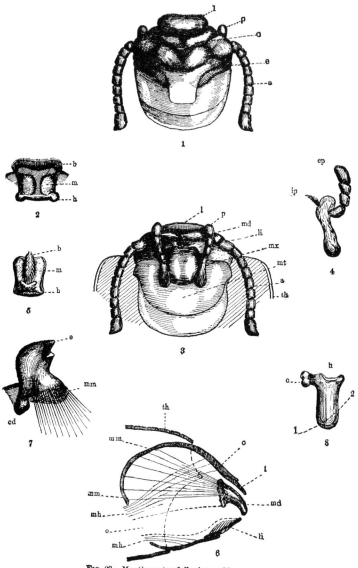

FIG. 23.—Mouth-parts of *Zopherus Mexicanus.*

glass jar at college, found no difficulty in cutting its way out, of an evening, through a covering of sheet-lead one six-teenth inch thick.

Of the common borers we may name a few of the more important. The Buprestids and the related beetles are well

FIG. 24.—Buprestid.   FIG. 25.—Pine-weevil.   FIG. 26.—Clytus.

recognized as among the most destructive and most numer-ous; a number of species, represented in Fig. 24 by *Buprestis Virginica*, living in pine timbers. The grub of the hand-some Painted Clytus, so common among the flowers of the golden-rod, infests locust-trees, that of the *Clytus speciosa* is destructive to maples. Although the Weevils are usually spoken of as the fruit and grain destroyers, their reputation seems equally bad among timbers. One of the most common of beetles, represented by numbers of species, we find them infesting every kind of tree from bark to heart-wood, and especially destructive to felled timbers. It is to a species of

EXPLANATION OF FIGURE 23.

1. Dorsal aspect of the head of *Zopherus Mexicanus:* *l*, labrum ; *p*, palpus ; *c*, clypeus ; *e*, eye ; *a*, antenna.
2. Inner face of the labrum : *b*, fringing bristles ; *m*, insertion of muscles ; *h*, deep hinge, with insertion of muscles joining to clypeus.
3. Ventral aspect of the head : *l*, labrum ; *p*, palpus ; *md*, mandible ; *li*, labium ; *mx*, maxilla ; *mt*, mentum ; *a*, antenna ; *th*, thorax.
4. Ventral aspect of the left maxilla with its palpi : *ep*, external palpus ; *ip*, internal palpus.
5. Inner face of the labium : *b*, bristles of tongue-groove ; *m*, insertion of tongue-muscles ; *h*, hinge, connecting the labium with the mentum.
6. Longitudinal-vertical section of the head : *th*, thorax ; *c*, clypeus ; *l*, labrum ; *md*, man-dible ; *li*, labium ; *mm*, muscles of the mandible ; *mh*, muscles moving the head on the thorax ; *o*, œsophagus.
7. Ventral aspect of the right mandible : *e*, cutting edge ; *cd*, double-headed pivot or con-dyle ; *mm*, insertion of the muscles.
8. External lateral aspect of the right mandible : *h*, the hinge ; *c*, the condyle ; 1, 2, direc-tion of cutting movement.

From the Journal of the New York Microscopical Society, July, 1888.

weevil we are indebted for the worm-eaten appearance pre-
sented by old carved-oak furniture. So often, indeed, are
these borings regarded as an evidence of the antiquity of
furniture, that many European dealers have been known to
imitate their presence by a charge of fine bird-shot.

The large Roebuck beetle, or Horn-bug (*Lucanus dama,*

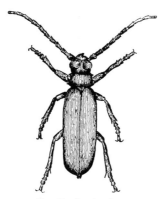

Fig. 27.—Saw-beetle.   Fig. 28.—Horn-bug.

Fig. 28), is fortunately at present rather uncommon; the
grub attains the size of a man's thumb after a six years' life
spent in boring forest trees.

Another large borer is the common brown Saw-Beetle
(*Prionus unicolor*), named from its saw-like feelers. It infests pine-trees, and may be
taken as the type of the destructive saw-beetle family.

Fig. 29.—Carpenter-bee.

Besides the beetles nearly
every other order of insects
has members more or less destructive as borers. Among
wasps, for example, we are
surely all familiar with the
large Carpenter - Bee (*Xylo-
carpa Virginica*), so common
about the posts and railings

of our country porches, which bores a gallery for its young large enough to admit a finger.

Fig. 30.—Carpenter-moth.

As another example we may mention a moth, not uncommon about the city, whose caterpillar lives in the hard yellow locust, the Carpenter-Moth (*Xyleutes robiniæ*).

Before closing, it would perhaps be of interest to say a few words of the relation of insects to **knarls** or **burls.** These knotty outgrowths may occur on any tree, both on branch and trunk, but become valuable only when of a size suitable for cabinet-work or veneer-cutting.' The wood in such cases is abnormally hard, is dark and mottled in color, and usually presents a curled, wavy grain.

The origin of burls has as yet been but little studied. It is, however, usually conceded that these deformations, like the well-understood galls, were originally produced by insects; that the young grubs feeding upon and irritating the most delicate tissues, have caused the plant to form the **irregular accumulation** of new wood-cells, both in and about **the injured** part. That this formation will go on for ages after the cause has disappeared seems to have been well established, and it is often found that in after-years the burl may fail to exhibit the slightest trace of its insect origin.

As in the formation of galls, the insects that cause these deformations are not confined to an isolated group, but belong to a number of families in no less than five different orders. The beetle-larvæ, namely, Buprestids and Weevils, are usually regarded as the typical burl-formers.

PRESERVATION OF WOOD.

To preserve wood it must be protected from those causes which induce warping, checking, and discoloration; be removed from those conditions which favor the development of fungi and the boring of insects.

Attention must first be given to the seasoning of the wood. The logs should be sawed into lumber as soon as possible after cutting, or, if they have been immersed in water, immediately on removal from the water, then stacked in the open air and allowed to remain until thoroughly seasoned, or be subjected to some other drying process now in use. If the logs are to be shipped a long distance, or remain unsawed for even a few weeks, it is necessary to remove the bark and coat the surface, particularly the ends of the log, with a thick coat of tar or paint, to retard evaporation. From most logs the sap-wood should be removed, to prevent the attacks of fungi and insects. The sap-wood of lignum-vitæ is allowed to remain, to prevent checking in the heart-wood.

Exposure of the raw surface of wood to the alternate action of rain or moisture and sunlight causes a discoloration called **weather-stain**, which penetrates into the tissue and renders the surface unfit for finished work. If exposed for a long time, the softer portions are worn away, giving a **weather-beaten** effect. To protect smoothed boards from the action of the weather, they are oiled, painted, or varnished. Sawed and weather-beaten surfaces require a large quantity of paint to cover them, and may be whitewashed or coated with some other lime preparation.

Few woods can resist the constant alternation of dampness and dryness occurring in those portions of timber in contact with the soil. Here we have the most favorable condition for the attacks of fungi and eventually decay or rot. The ends of beams and joists resting on damp walls, posts set in stone foundations, fences and railroad-ties, are well-known examples of wood exposed to this condition. Those woods which have the least tendency to decay in contact with the soil are the cypress, redwood, cedar, locust, and white oak. The others require some one of the various artificial means to preserve them.

Charring, in which the wood is held for a few minutes in a fire until the surface is evenly and completely converted into charcoal. This will be effectual only in well-seasoned woods, because, if the wood checks after the operation, fungus-spores may germinate in the check and cause rotting of the wood. A specimen observed by the author had a large, well-developed polypore in a stick that had been charred only one year.

Creosote.—The protective substance developed in charring seems to be creosote, which is one of the best preservatives we have. The ends of timbers are placed in the creosote until they have drawn up into their pores a sufficient quantity, and, as long as it gives a perceptible odor to the wood, fungi and insects, including even the white ants, leave it alone.

Wood-Tar and **Coal-Tar** are quite frequently used in America as preserving coats for wood. They are to be recommended as cheap and effective, and especially adapted to out-of-door structures.

Paint.—Although the so-called metallic paint, in which an oxide of iron is the basis, and common paint, with carbonate of lead as a basis, have been used to a great extent for preserving wood, they are desirable only for those portions of wooden structures not in contact with the soil. In any event, they need renewal every two or three years to continue their preservative action.

Many chemical solutions have been used to protect wood from fungi, insects, and even from fire. Of these a ten-percent solution of sulphate of copper, in which the wood is placed until its cells and vessels have absorbed a sufficient quantity, is the most prominent. A mixture, of one part of silicate of sodium and three of water, applied to the wood, renders it fire-proof and free from the attacks of parasites. Acid solutions of various alums, together with sulphates of zinc and potassium, have been strongly recommended. For railroad-ties a solution of rosin and paraffin in benzine has been used effectually. In most of these solutions the wood is simply immersed; but, to render the absorption very complete, the air is first removed by vacuum-pumps, and the wood then immersed in the preserving fluid.

Wood will not decay as long as it is kept well ventilated and dry. It may become brittle with age, but no sign of fungus growth will make its appearance. This is shown in the wood of old pieces of furniture and the interior woodwork of houses, which the coat of paint or varnish has kept perfectly sound.

The opposite condition, in which the wood is constantly covered by water, will also preserve it; as examples of this, we have the oak of vessels sunken for a hundred years or more, and the remains of ancient lake-dwellers in Switzerland and England. It is because of this peculiar preservative action of water that foundations of great structures of granite and marble are laid upon the tops of wooden piles, driven below the low-water mark.

In America, with its bountiful supply of wood, which is easily obtained and cheap, little attention has been paid to means of preserving it. But now we begin to note the result of extravagant and unchecked destruction of timber-lands by the increasing scarcity of some of the ordinary kinds, and in the attempts made to preserve railroad-ties.

PART SECOND.

TOOLS—DRAWING—EXERCISES.

WOOD-WORKING.

In arranging a workshop, the position of the work-bench with regard to the light is of prime importance. For carpentry and general joinery, the light should be at the head of the bench, so that it can pass under the try-square, and to avoid awkward positions in testing work. The turner and carver should have the light come down on the top of their work, from a sky-light, or have the lathe or bench in front of a tall window, the lower part of which is screened by tool-racks.

Although some workmen are obliged to keep their tools in chests for convenience in moving, or in drawers under the bench, the better plan is to have them in a closet within easy reach, above the bench or against the wall opposite the bench. The closet should have the doors and sides furnished with strips of wood notched to hold the various tools, nearly all of which may be supported on such racks. Each tool thus has its own peg or place, in which it is kept when not in use. Even in a chest or in drawers the saws, chisels, gouges, bits, and other edge tools, are separated by notched strips to prevent injury to their edges.

The work-bench itself, made of hard wood, preferably maple, requires some care to preserve a smooth and clean top. The saws, chisels, boring-tools, nails, screws, or other sharp tools, must never cut into the bench. The vise should be brought square to its work, and no irregular or metallic objects should be fastened in it. Frequently brush the top of the bench and clean off drops of glue, paint, or varnish, immediately. Make no pencil-marks on the top, as they soil the work.

Have on the bench only those tools to be used in the work at hand ; all others must be put away.

The tools should be used only for the purpose for which they are intended ; measures and marking-tools not to be used as levers, the try-square not as a hammer or screw-driver, nor the compasses as a boring-tool.

The polished surfaces of steel tools should be carefully protected from moisture and especially from perspiration. To prevent rust, rub the bright parts frequently with a mixture of paraffine and vaseline, or equal parts of beeswax and tallow. If rust should appear, brighten the spot with some fine emery-cloth and oil, rubbing always in the direction of the polish scratches.

In working up old material, the greatest caution must be taken to prevent sawing and planing on nails, etc.

In mortising, do not strike the chisel with the hammer, and on no occasion strike the hammer on its side. Planes must have their soles frequently rubbed with the wax or paraffine mixture ; always lay them on their side or on thin strips on the bench.

The student should wear a long apron, without pockets, and made of strong material. Workmen use short aprons, and while building or in out-of-door work have the bottom turned up and sewed, to make a large pocket for nails and small tools.

The work must be carefully protected from bruises by dropping, striking with hammer or other tools, and from chips on the bench.

In all this training three things are to be aimed at : First, *accuracy*, which in wood-working specially applies to marking and cutting ; second, *finish*, or smoothness ; and, third, *quickness* of execution.

After marking out the work, it should be inspected and approved by the instructor before cuts are made. Pencil-marks must always be light and fine, so as to be easily removed.

When an exercise is finished, the work should have the name or number of the student and the date written on it, the bench brushed off, and all tools cleaned and put away.

Tools. (Plate A.)

The following are the ordinary measuring, marking, and holding tools :

1. Four-fold, *two-foot* rule. The graduations of inches and even fractions of an inch running from right to left.

2. Full size of portion of inside divided into, *a*, sixteenths ; *b*, one of the scales usually found on the carpenter's rule. It is the three-quarter inch to one foot scale.

3. Portion of the metric rule. This rule is one *meter* long, divided into ten segments, each one *decimeter*, which is divided into ten *centimeters*, and each centimeter into ten *millimeters*, or thousandths of a meter.

4. Full size of one end of the metric rule. Note that the centimeters are numbered from left to right.

5. A circle is divided into three hundred and sixty degrees ; a quarter-circle, *a*, has ninety degrees, and measures a right or *square* angle. The arc, *b*, measures a thirty degrees opening ; *c*, forty-five degrees ; *d*, sixty degrees.

6. Carpenter's *steel square*, used for measuring and marking timber ; the long side twenty-four inches, the short side sixteen ; the outer edges graduated into sixteenths, the inner into quarters or eighths.

7. *Try-square*, rosewood handle faced with brass, steel blade.

8. Small steel square for testing fine work.

9. Sliding *T-bevel*, for marking or testing other than a square angle.

10. Carpenters use three sizes of pencils : a short stick of plumbago, three quarters inch square, a large pencil (see section), and an ordinary No. 3.

11. *Bench-knife ;* at *a*, round taper-point for scratching ; at *b*, a knife-edge. 12. *Marking-gauge :* *a*, the bar ; *b*, the head.

13. Spring *compasses*. 14. *Plumb-bob* and line.

15. *Spirit-level :* *a* for horizontal, *b* for vertical surfaces.

16. *Bench-vise :* *a, bench-screw*. The vise is adjusted by the screw and a strip containing holes or notches, fastened to the bottom of the vise.

17. *Bench-stop* of hard maple, about two inches square. There is a great variety of iron bench-stops.

18. Pine *bench-hook*. 19. Iron *bench-dog*. 20. Iron *clamp*.

21. *Hand-screw*. 22. *Oil-stone*. 23. *Oil-slip*. 24. *Oil-can*.

25. *Miter-box* with one side projecting to catch against the bench-top. 26. *Glue-pot :* *a*, for the water ; *b*, for the glue.

27. Carpenter's *horse*.

Plate A.

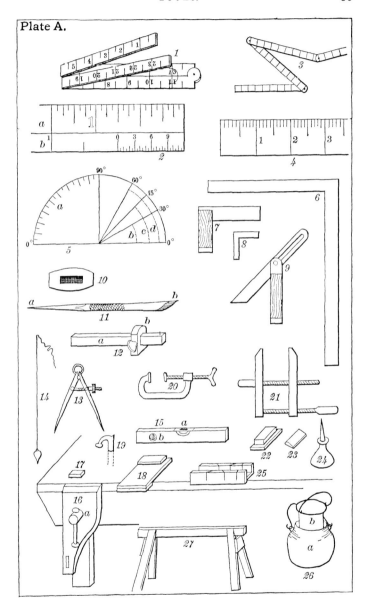

Tools. (Plate B.)

The chief edge-tools used by the carpenter are :

1. *Rip-saw* and *cross-cut*, apple-wood or beech handles and steel blades.

2. *Compass-saw.*

3. *Back-saw*, a very thin blade stiffened by an iron or brass back. Also called tenon-saw.

4. *Frame-saw.*

5. *Float*, like a saw, but with wide teeth.

6. *Chisel*, with apple-wood or hickory handle, a bevel side, and a flat side or face.

7. *Gouge*, the face is the hollow side.

8. *Jack-plane:* a, stock ; b, top ; c, sole, in front• the toe and behind the heel ; d, handle ; e, wedge, driven behind the throat ; f, iron. There are three large planes used by carpenters : jack-plane, sixteen inches long, sometimes furnished with a single iron ; *fore-plane*, twenty-two inches long; and *jointer*, twenty-six or more inches in length. 9. *Plane-iron.*

10. *Cap.*   11. *Double iron*, cap and iron united.

12. *Wedge.*   13. *Smoothing-plane.*

14. *Rabbet-plane*, of which there are several forms, some with irons the full width of the sole, some with a small side cutter, and some with stops.   15. Iron of rabbet-plane.

16, 17. Show the shapes of paring *match-planes.*

18, 19. Shapes of match-plane irons.

20. Shape of the sole of a *hollow.*

21. Shape of a *round.*   22. Shape of a *sash-plane.*

23. *Plow;* recent form with iron stock and apple-wood handle ; a, iron, secured by a thumb-screw ; b, *fence; c, stop* for regulating depth of cut ; d, handle.   24. One of the set of irons.

25. The sole with its iron, which when attached to the stock makes a fillister or rabbet-plane.

26. *Scratch-plane* for preparing wood before gluing.

27. Portion of the scratch-plane iron, showing its teeth, full size.

28. *Brace*, with head, handle, and bit-holder.   29. *Twist-bit.*

30. *Center-bit.*   31. *Auger-bit.*   32. *Rose countersink.*

33, 34. *Half-round reamer.*   35. *Draw-knife.*

36. *Spoke-shave.*   37. *Screw-driver.*   38. *Claw-hammer.*

39. *Bench-ax.*   40. Wooden *mallet.*

Besides which there are rasps, files, brad-awls, and many other tools for special purposes.

Plate B.

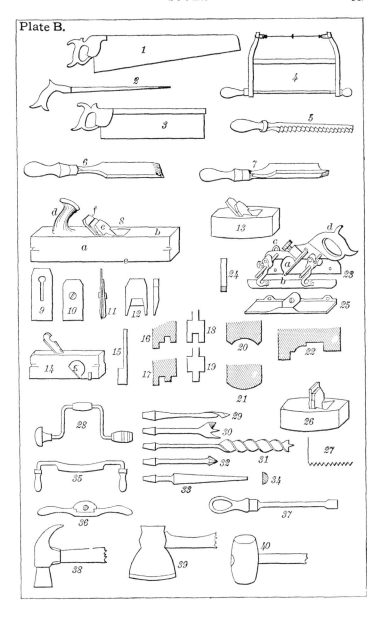

Drawing. (Plate C.)

The distance between the heavy lines in Fig. 1, measured according to the scale, three quarters of an inch to one foot, will be found to be 2 feet 3¾ inches. This measurement may be expressed by using the signs for feet and inches, or by writing a letter on the line and referring to the margin or notes for its value. Broken lines usually terminated by arrow-heads are used to show the extent of the measurement.

In locating a circle, give the distances of its center or circumference from two known points (Fig. 2). An oblique line must have both ends determined, or one end, its length, and inclination (Fig. 2).

The drawings of any object should consist of as many parts as are necessary to show all its dimensions. Usually three are sufficient, as in Fig. 3, in which a is the *elevation*, b the *plan*, and c the end-view or *side elevation*, of a rectangular block.

Sections through an object are frequently shown in drawings. If it is cut across the grain, it is shaded by straight parallel oblique lines, a and b, Fig. 4, which show two views of a section through the block, Fig. 3, on the line $e f$. Sections with the grain are shaded by lines parallel with the grain ; thus, a vertical section through the line $g h$ of Fig. 3 would appear as at c, Fig. 4.

Generally one perspective of an object will show a sufficient number of its details to enable a workman to understand its form. From a true perspective, as the cube in Fig. 5, measures can not be easily obtained ; therefore, in illustrating the following exercises, false or *parallel* perspective is employed.

Fig. 6 represents a cube drawn in right and left parallel perspective. It is seen that surfaces and lines parallel with the plane of the paper are drawn their full size and correct shape. The receding horizontal lines are represented by shorter lines inclined at an angle of 45°. To obtain this shortened length, the full length of the line is laid off on a vertical line drawn from the nearest end of the receding one, and from the upper end of the length thus obtained an oblique line at an angle of 30° is let fall ; where it intersects the 45° line is the shortened length, as shown in Fig. 6.

Fig. 7, a, b, and c show the elevations and plan of a work-bench, drawn to a scale of $\frac{1}{4}''$ to $1'$; d and e show the details of the vise, $\frac{1}{2}''$ to 1 . The irregular line-shading is used to represent wooden surfaces.

Plate C.

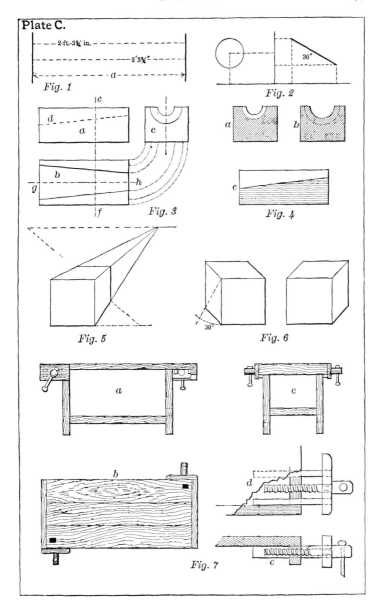

Fig. 1

Fig. 2

Fig. 3

Fig. 4

Fig. 5

Fig. 6

Fig. 7

Exercise 1.—Use of the Chisel.

Material.—A rough block of pine, about 2″ square, and 8″ long.
Work.—1. To cut one side of the block perfectly smooth and flat.
  2. To cut an adjacent side smooth, flat, and at right angles with the first side.

Fasten the block lengthwise in the vise, so that about $1\frac{1}{2}″$ of it is above the bench-top.

Hold the **chisel** in the right hand, the cutting edge obliquely to the direction of the grain, and inclined from the block a sufficient amount to make a thin shaving (*a, b*, Fig. 1). The fingers of the left hand should rest on the face of the blade, and guide the cutting edge. If additional strength is required to force the chisel through the wood, grasp the blade in the left hand.

The surface is **pared** smooth with the chisel in the above position. To make the surface flat, turn the chisel on its face, as shown in Fig. 2, *a* and *b ;* cut very thin shavings in those places where the wood is too high, and avoid cutting in the low places.

To test the surface, hold the try-square on various parts of the surface in the two positions, as shown in Fig. 3, *a* and *b*, and note the light passing under the square at the low places. Handle the try-square with the left hand. If its edge is pressed or rubbed against the wood, it will mark the high places. Look along the block from end to end, to see whether the surface is twisted or warped. Also pass the fingers lightly over the surface, to note its irregularities.

When smooth and flat, this surface of the block is called its **face.** Turn the block in the vise and fasten with its face outward. Pare the second side the same as the first, testing frequently for flatness. When nearly smooth and flat, remove the block and test the angle between the sides with the try-square, as shown in Fig. 4. Care must be taken to hold the try-square true to the face.

When the second side is finished, mark it and the face with a pencil, as shown in Fig. 4. The edge of the block, toward which the marks point, is the **face-edge**, from which all measures are made.

In using any sharp tool, care must be taken to avoid cutting the work-bench, the bench-stop, and particularly the hands. Always keep the hands behind the chisel-edge.

Ex. I.

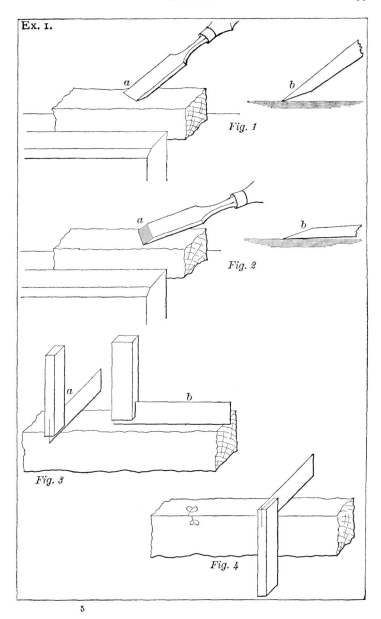

Fig. 1

Fig. 2

Fig. 3

Fig. 4

Exercise 2.—Use of the Chisel continued.

Work.—1. To mark the block of Exercise 1 for width of face.

2. To cut the remaining sides so that the block will be $1\frac{1}{2}''$ square.

3. To chamfer the edges.

Fasten the block in the vise with face up and face-edge outward. Hold the rule as shown in Fig. 1, so that it measures exactly $1\frac{1}{2}''$ from the face-edge, and make a small mark with the pencil along the end of the rule. Adjust the rule by bending the first finger of the left hand underneath it against the face-edge (Fig. 2), until the point of the pencil, held against the end of the rule, comes on the measured mark, and draw the rule and pencil along the block, producing a line parallel to and $1\frac{1}{2}''$ from the face-edge. Mark the side opposite to the face of the block in the same way.

Pare the third side down to the pencil marks, being careful not to pass below them. Mark and pare the fourth side.

In cutting **end-wood** with the chisel, considerable force is necessary to push and guide the tool. Small shavings must be cut at a time, and, in order to leave a smooth surface behind it, the cutting edge must be very sharp. Instead of cutting straight down, the cut is oblique, as shown by the arrow in Fig. 3, or the chisel is inclined and pushed in the direction of the arrow in Fig. 4. The block should rest on the bench-hook or a small waste board, in cutting the end-wood as above.

Lay out the **chamfer,** as shown in Fig. 5, $1''$ from the ends of the block, and $\frac{3}{8}''$ wide. Mark the lines parallel with the face-edge, with the rule and pencil, and the cross marks with the try-square. Lay out the ends of the chamfer according to the measures given in Figs. 6 and 7; the first is an **ogee,** and the second a **bevel.**

In cutting the chamfer, use the chisel in the position shown in Fig. 1, Ex. 1, and great care must be taken to avoid cutting beyond the pencil marks. Cut the ends after the straight portion is finished.

In Fig. 8 are shown some of the shapes given to chamfer ends.

Ex. 2.

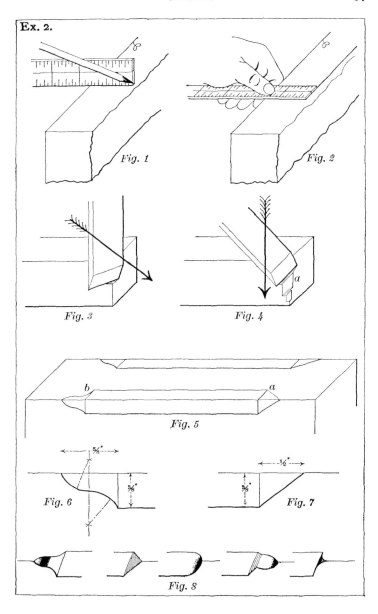

Fig. 1

Fig. 2

Fig. 3

Fig. 4

Fig. 5

Fig. 6

Fig. 7

Fig. 8

Exercise 3.—Use of the Gouge.

Material.—A block of dressed pine, 2″ wide, 1¼″ thick, and about 6″ long.

Work.—To shape a molding with gouge and chisel.

Lay out the block as shown in Fig. 1, using the measures as given in Fig. 2. The form of the molding, an ogee, as seen on the end of the block, *a*, Fig. 1, is sketched on the wood, or, as is the practice in shops, is marked on the end from a thin pattern, Fig. 2. The lines *b, b,* Fig. 1, are **drawn** by the rule and pencil.

In cutting with the **gouge,** apply the same directions given for the use of the chisel. Cut small shavings, hold the gouge obliquely, as shown in Fig. 3, test frequently with the try-square, and avoid cutting beyond the marks. The hollow portion should be cut first with the gouge, then the small rectangular piece in the upper part of the molding cut out with the chisel, leaving what is called a **quirk,** and lastly the top rounded by the chisel. In cutting the quirk, the chisel is held by the blade and drawn along the pencil mark on the top of the block, cutting like a knife-edge, and the wood pared down to the bottom of the cut; the chisel is then again used like a knife, and more pared off, this process being repeated until the entire quirk is cut.

To **return** the molding, the end is given the same form as the face, *a*, Fig. 4. This form may be marked on the end, from a piece of molding held against it, by the marking-point of the bench-knife, or by measuring points along the curve with the rule, and marking through them with the pencil. The return is cut down upon a waste board with the gouge and chisel. In cutting across the grain with the gouge, it must have a circular motion, which is the same in effect as the oblique cut of the chisel.

In drawings, the form of a molding is always indicated by a section of it, as shown at *c*, Fig. 4.

In Fig. 5 is represented a core-box, made by pattern-makers. It is an example of gouge work.

Fig. 6 shows a molding **coped,** or fitted to another. The shape of the end of a molding for coping may be obtained by sawing the end in a miter-box.

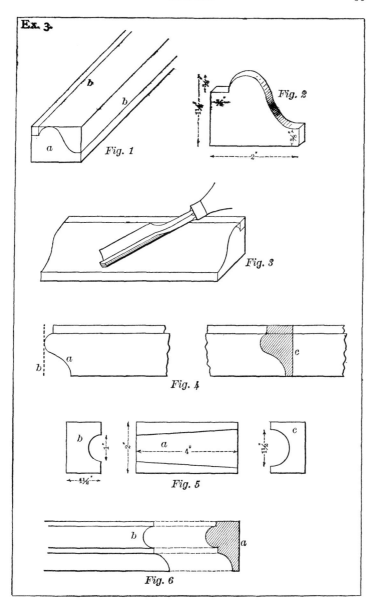

Fig. 1

Fig. 2

Fig. 3

Fig. 4

Fig. 5

Fig. 6

Exercise 4.—Use of the Hammer.

Material.—Sawed block of pine, 4″ square and 16″ long.
Work.—To strike blows on the block, in order to learn the right
   manner of holding the hammer.

Grasp the handle of the **hammer** firmly, whether for a light or
a heavy blow, and hold it so that its striking face is parallel with
the surface of the wood (Fig. 1).   Strike two or three light blows
at one end of the block, and examine the impressions, which should
be like those of *a*, Fig. 2 ; but if like *b*, Fig. 2, the hammer must
be held better.   Strike two or three again, and examine the prints
of the hammer.   Now strike several heavy blows, and note the result.   It is a common fault among students to draw the handle
down, as in *a*, Fig. 3, in striking a hard blow, and in correcting
this fault to give the opposite result (*b*, Fig. 3).   If the print shows
that the hammer falls as at *c*, Fig. 3, then it is not held sufficiently
tight in the hand.

For light blows a wrist motion is used, for ordinary blows a
movement from the elbow, and for heavy blows a shoulder or combined movement of all the parts of the arm is necessary.

Cut nails are wedge-shaped, and if driven the wrong way will
spread the fibers and cause the wood to split; but if driven the
right way, break and compress the fibers without splitting the wood :
a and *b*, Fig. 4, show the cut nail in its proper position, *c* and *d*,
Fig. 4, the wrong position.   Pick up a cut nail near the smaller
end, the thumb and finger will instantly determine the wedge from
the parallel sides and place the nail properly on the wood.   Some
men pick up the nail near the larger end, but allow the third finger
to determine its shape.   Wire nails do not need examination before striking, but must be struck a direct blow, or they will bend.

Fig. 5 illustrates a peculiar drawn blow of the hammer.   Starting at *d*, it follows the direction of the broken line in its course ;
the effect of which is to bend the nail in such a manner that it
forces the board *a* close up to *c*, as shown at *f*.   This blow is prac-
ticed in nailing floors and clinching wrought nails.   If the point *a*,
Fig. 6, be struck light, drawn blows, it will curl, as shown at *b*.
And if the blows are now drawn less, but made harder, the point
will sink into the wood as at *d*, leaving a small and clean depression.

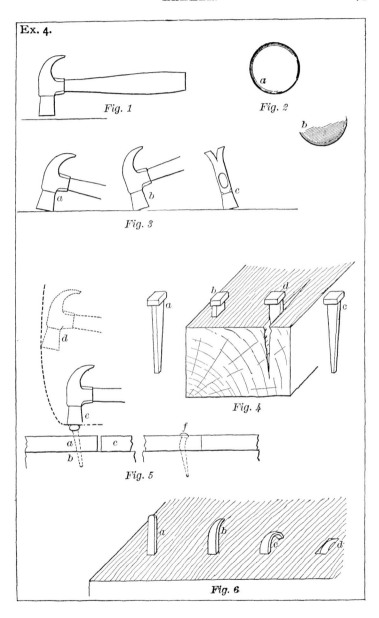

Ex. 4.

Fig. 1

Fig. 2

Fig. 3

Fig. 4

Fig. 5

Fig. 6

Exercise 5.—Use of the Jack-Plane.

Material.—The block used in the previous exercise.
Work.—1. To adjust the iron of the plane.
  2. To plane two adjacent surfaces flat and square.

In adjusting a **plane,** hold it in the left hand, with the thumb in the throat and pressed against the iron, as in Fig. 1. Look along the sole and note the projection of the iron, as at *a*, Fig. 2. The iron should be highest in the middle, and gradually curving until it disappears near the edges of the sole, as shown at *a*, Fig. 3. If it projects too far, strike the plane lightly on the hard **start,** *c*, Fig. 1, until it recedes the required amount. If the iron does not project far enough, strike its top, *a*, Fig. 1. If the iron projects too much on one side, strike the iron near the top on the project-ing side. When the iron is properly adjusted, give the wedge a light blow to secure the iron. The block may be fastened in the vise.

Hold the plane straight on the work, the left hand placed in front of the iron, properly, with the thumb on top and the fingers on the side. Stand firmly on the floor, with the right side close up to the bench, behind the block. At the beginning of the stroke, press down with the left hand only; at the finish, remove the left and press with the right. Each shaving should be the entire length of the block.

Examine the cut made by the iron; it may be either too deep or too shallow. If the cut surface is rough (*a*, Fig. 5), then the plane is working against the grain, and the block must be turned around. If smooth, as in Fig. 6, it is cutting with the grain. If the shavings do not curl in coming out of the throat, examine the position of the end of the cap; for the jack-plane $\frac{1}{8}''$ to $\frac{1}{4}''$ back is proper, and for other planes about $\frac{1}{16}''$ (*b*, Fig. 5, and *c*, Fig. 6).

Plane out all the saw marks or weather stains, and examine the surface for flatness and warping, as in Exercise 1. Plane and square the adjacent side, and mark the face-edge.

In planing a warped board, the plane is sometimes pushed ob-liquely across the board, as shown by the arrows in Fig. 7, until flat, and then finished with straight strokes.

Ex. 5.

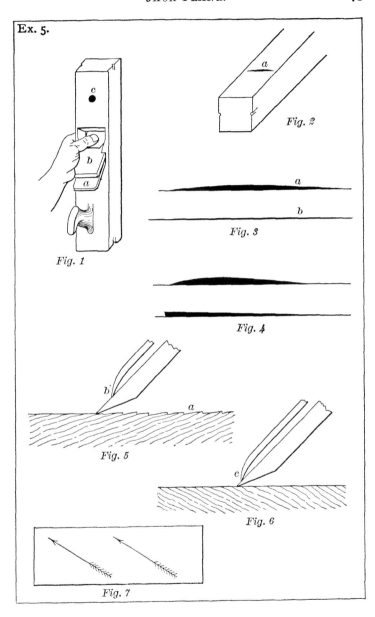

Fig. 1

Fig. 2

Fig. 3

Fig. 4

Fig. 5

Fig. 6

Fig. 7

Exercise 6.—Plane continued, and Marking-Gauge.

Material.—Same as before.

Work.—1. To smooth the two planed surfaces of the block with the smoothing-plane.

    2. To mark with the gauge for the third side.

    3. To plane the third and fourth sides of the block.

The **smoothing-plane** is adjusted the same as the jack-plane, excepting that its iron is drawn back by a blow on the back of the stock. Its iron should just show, as in *b*, Fig. 3, Ex. 5, and should remove a very thin shaving. Smooth the face and adjacent side of the block, testing with the try-square, and marking over again the face-edge.

Adjust the gauge, holding it in the left hand, thumb on the head; move the bar so that the marking-point is exactly $3\frac{1}{2}''$ from the head; fasten the bar with the thumb-screw. In marking, hold the head in the left hand, thumb against the bar near the point (*a*, Fig. 1). Incline the gauge as shown in the figure, until it makes a faint mark; press the head of the gauge firmly against the face-edge, and mark the entire length of the block. Repeat, making the mark deeper, until it is sufficiently distinct. If the head of the gauge is not pressed against the face-edge, or if the point is forced in deeply at first, it is apt to follow the grain, as shown in Fig. 2, where the gauge makes a fault from *a* to *b*. Gauge all around $3\frac{1}{2}''$ from the face of the block, as shown in Fig. 3.

Plane the edges of the third side down to the gauge-marks, as in Fig. 4; these beveled surfaces serve as guides. Then plane down the middle, being very careful not to go beyond the gauge-marks.

Fig. 5 shows the manner of truing the edge of a board by using one side of the edge of the plane-iron. In the figure, *c* is the stock, *a* the high part of the edge. The fingers of the left hand are used as a guide, and pass along the side of the board at *b*.

Fig. 6 shows one of the best forms of modern planes; its adjustments are made with screws and levers: *a* and *b* fasten the iron, *c* moves the iron sideways, *d* regulates the depth of the cut, *e* is the iron, and *f* its cap.

Ex. 6.

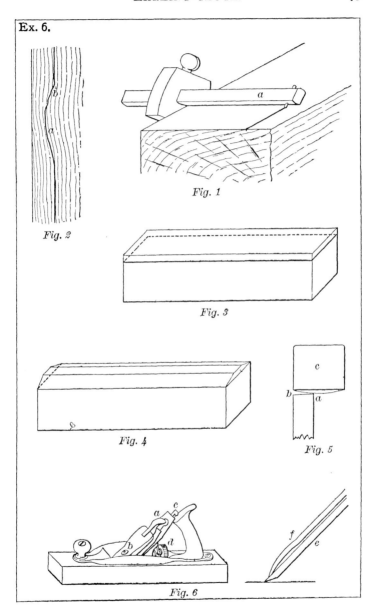

Fig. 2

Fig. 1

Fig. 3

Fig. 4

Fig. 5

Fig. 6

Exercise 7.—Use of the Rip-Saw.

Material.—Squared block of the previous exercises.
Work.—To saw the block into boards which may be planed to ¼″
    thick.

Examine the **rip-saw**; note that its teeth are about four and
a half to an inch; the angular opening 60°, and the slant of the
tooth about 90° to the direction of the cut. In Fig. 1 the teeth
are shown slanting toward the point, and are called **hooked**. At *a*,
Fig. 2, the teeth are square, and at *b* are **raked**. The teeth are
smaller near the point of the saw. The face of the teeth may be
cut square across, as at *a*, Fig. 3, or obliquely as at *b*. In order
that the saw may not **bind**, its teeth are **set**—that is, the points are

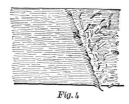

Fig. 4.

bent, as at *a*, *b*, *c*, Fig. 3, alternately to one
side and the other. The effect of the teeth
on the wood-fibers shows that the action is
tearing. Fig. 4 exhibits a magnified view
of a section through a saw-**kerf**.

Gauge all around the block ½″ from its
face. Fasten the block vertically in the
vise with its face outward. Hold the saw
firmly in the right hand, against the thumb of the left acting as
a guide (*a*, Fig. 7), and about ⅛″ beyond the gauge-mark. Move
the saw with short strokes, back and forth, a little above the wood;
let it gradually approach and enter the wood. The weight of the
saw must be sustained by the right hand while starting; after it
has entered fairly into the wood, let the saw cut by its own weight.
Go slowly, and push the saw as straightly as possible. When the
saw has penetrated as far as shown at *a*, Fig. 8, change to the opposite side and saw down as shown at *b ;* change again, and continue this alternation, keeping the saw all the while about ⅛″ from
the gauge-mark.

In starting the saw, many workmen would begin at *b*, Fig. 7,
and draw the saw backward, resting on the wood. The saw cuts
quickest if pushed at right angles to the grain, but if inclined, as
in Fig. 6, requires less force. In sawing boards, use the horses for
supports and test the position of the saw, as shown in Fig. 5, until
practice gives a correct habit.

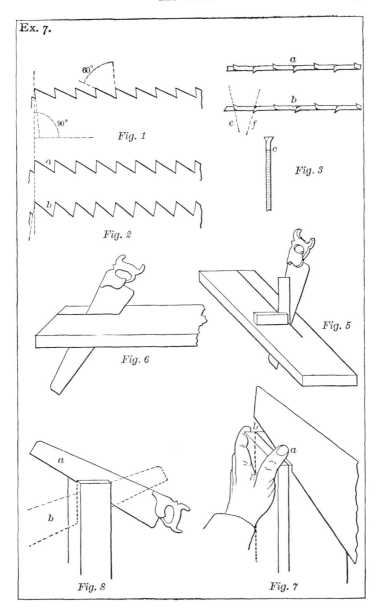

Ex. 7.

Fig. 1

Fig. 2

Fig. 3

Fig. 5

Fig. 6

Fig. 8

Fig. 7

Exercise 8.—Use of the Cross-Cut.

Material.—Block of pine, 4″ square and 16″ long.
Work.—1. Plane the block to 3¾″ square.
    2. Practice sawing with cross-cut.

Examine the **cross-cut,** and note the small, pointed teeth, shown enlarged at *a*, Fig. 1 ; look down on the tops of the teeth ; they appear as at *b*, Fig. 1 ; look along the saw from the handle toward the point ; a depression is seen, made by the peculiar shape and set of the points of the teeth (*c*, Fig. 1).

Plane the block carefully to 3¾″ square, observing instruction in Exercises 5 and 6.

Measure and mark a point on the face-edge, ½″ from the right end. Hold the try-square, as shown at *a*, Fig. 2, firmly against the face-edge and coinciding with the pencil-mark. Draw a pencil-mark along the try-square. Then place the try-square in the position shown at *b*, Fig. 2, and again mark along the square.

Place the block on the bench-hook, with the marks toward you (Fig. 3). Hold the saw as directed in the previous exercise, the thumb used as a guide, and start the cut in the same way, beginning at the front or back of the face and on the pencil-mark. Let the weight of the saw do the cutting ; give all your attention to guiding. Avoid letting the point of the saw drop at the end of the stroke. Keep the movement of the teeth as parallel as possible with the bench-top. Examine the sawed surface.

Repeat the exercise, this time using the knife for marking, and guiding the saw so that the kerf is to the right of the knife-mark.

Fig. 6

In Fig. 4, *a* represents the knife-mark and *c* the kerf. Repeat again, this time sawing to the left of the knife-mark, as at *b*, Fig. 4 ; this last piece should be exactly ½″ thick. Repeat the exercise with oblique cuts, as shown in Fig. 5, always measuring and adjusting the try-square on the face-edge. Fig. 6 shows the appearance under the microscope of a section of pine-wood which has been sawed by a cross-cut. The fibers are bent and broken by the sharp points, showing the tearing action of the tool.

Ex. 8.

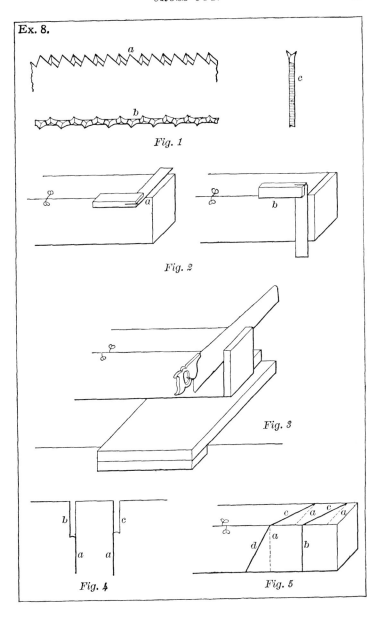

Fig. 1

Fig. 2

Fig. 3

Fig. 4

Fig. 5

Sharpening Tools. (Plate D.)

To sharpen or *whet* a chisel, moisten the *oil-stone* with a few drops of oil; hold the chisel by the blade in the right hand, as shown in Fig. 1, two or three fingers of the left pressing on the face of the chisel near the edge, *a*. The chisel is moved backward and forward the entire length of the stone, and maintained strictly at a certain angle, about 30° to 35°, depending on the kind of chisel and the work to be done with it: for paring, thinner angles, and for mortising, thicker angles are used.

In the forward movement (*a* to *b*, Fig. 2), the tool must be pressed hard on the stone, but lightly as it is drawn back ; and the surface formed at the cutting edge should be flat, as shown at *c*.

Avoid a rocking motion, as shown in Fig. 3, in which the tool is started at too great an angle (*a*), which becomes less as it moves along, ending in an angle much too small, as at *c*. This fault, which is a very common one, gives to the edge a curved shape, as shown at *d*, Fig. 3.

After the stone has worn the steel down to the edge, the chisel is turned on its face, flat on the stone, and moved forward lightly once or twice to remove the *wire-edge* caused by the grinding.

To sharpen a plane-iron, hold it the same as the chisel, turned so as to bring the corners of the iron within the limits of the stone ; press with considerable force in the forward strokes, and keep the iron strictly at its proper angle, about 35°.

The iron of the jack-plane must have a rocking motion sidewise, so as to preserve its curved edge.

When the stone is small or narrow, a circular motion is given to the iron, as at *a*, Fig. 4. For the finishing touches, the iron is pushed forward lightly, raised from the stone coming back, and removing the wire-edge, as in the case of the chisel.

To sharpen a gouge, hold it and the *oil-slip* as shown in Fig. 5. Give the slip a back-and-forward motion while the tool is turned to bring all parts of the edge to bear on the stone. Remove the wire-edge with the round side of the slip.

Should the surface of the oil-stone become hollow or uneven, it may be made flat by grinding with fine sand or medium emery on a flat stone or cast-iron plate. To remove oil which has hardened in the pores of the surface, the stone may be placed in boiling, soapy water, or in some strong alkaline solution.

Plate **D.**

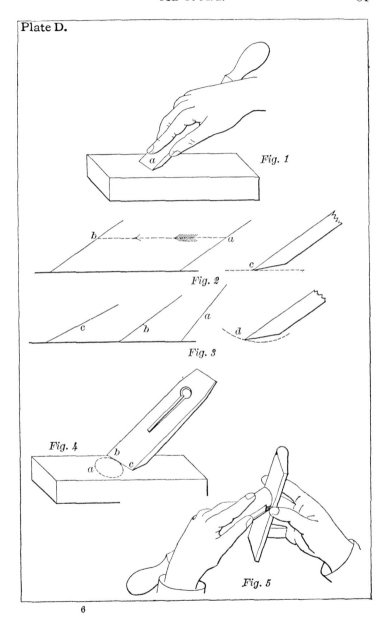

Fig. 1

Fig. 2

Fig. 3

Fig. 4

Fig. 5

Sharpening Tools. (Plate E.)

ON THE GRINDSTONE.

The *grindstone* must be kept constantly wet with water while in use. Of the many positions in which the tool may be held against the grindstone, that shown at *a*, Fig. 1, is the easiest for a student. The handle, held in the right hand, rests on a board at *b*, the bevel is pressed against the stone at *c*, with the palm of the left hand, which is applied to the face of the tool. The angle of the ground surface is regulated by moving the handle nearer to or away from the stone.

At *d*, Fig. 1, the angle of the bevel is regulated by moving the handle on the rest, and maintained by a finger held against the rest. At *e*, Fig. 1, and *b*, Fig, 2, are shown positions used by workmen.

The tool must not be held on one part of the stone, but constantly moved so as to wear the face of the stone evenly, as shown at *a*, Fig 2.

For chisels, gouges, and planes, the angle is tested by a gauge, shown full size in Fig. 3, made of steel or brass, with an opening of 20° to 25°, as shown at *c*, the value of the opening stamped on the gauge, and a hole at one end for a small chain fastened to the grindstone-frame. The bevel of the tool, *b*, is placed in the opening, *c*, and its angle tested ; if too thin, the handle, *b*, Fig. 1, must be drawn away from the stone, or brought nearer if too thick. When once determined a mark may be made on the rest at *b*, and the grinding continued until the bevel is brought down to the face. The edge is then tested with the try-square.

Care must be taken to preserve the correct shape of plane-irons (see *a*, *b*, Fig. 3, Ex. 5), and particularly the edge, which must be square.

Gouges are ground as shown in Fig. 4, so that the edge slants, and is square to the whetted surface, as shown by *c*, *d*, Fig. 4. For special work some gouges are ground just the opposite to the ordinary tool—that is, with the edge on the outer surface, at *b*, instead of *a*, Fig. 4.

Fig. 5 represents a simple means of obtaining the bevel surface on a chisel. It is supported on the rest, *b*, and held against the side of an emery-wheel. The wheel should be constantly oiled or wet with water.

To remove hollows or grooves in the grindstone, hold a wrought-iron bar, pointing downward, resting on the support *b*, Fig. 1, and with its end cutting into the high parts of the face ; after which, smooth the stone by holding a coarse sandstone against it.

Plate E.

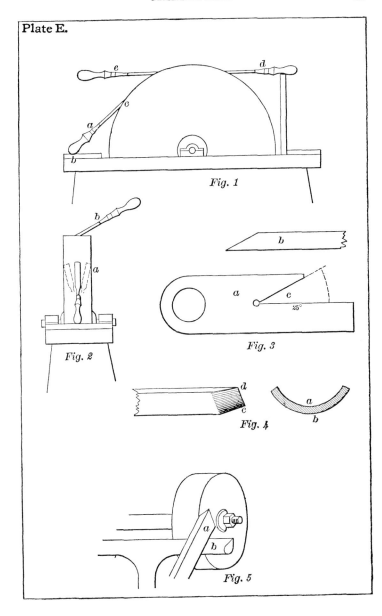

Fig. 1

Fig. 2

Fig. 3

Fig. 4

Fig. 5

Sharpening Tools. (Plate F.)

SAW-FILING.

The easiest saw to file is the rip-saw, with teeth square across and standing at 90°. Fasten the saw in the clamps as shown in Fig. 1. Pass a flat, smooth file lightly over the teeth first, to reduce all the tops to the same level. Examine the teeth carefully, and determine by the amount removed from the points which of them need the most filing, and whether on the square or beveled side. If the teeth are spaced irregularly, each filing should tend to correct the fault.

The *triangular file* is held in the right hand, its point guided by the thumb and forefinger of the left. For filing large teeth the file should have slanting furrows (*b*, Fig. 2) ; for small teeth, finer and less oblique furrows (*c*, Fig. 2). Pressure is applied only during the forward stroke of the file, it being raised above the tooth or touching very lightly as it comes back, because the brittle cutting edges, which are shaped as at *a*, Fig. 2, are easily rubbed off, and the file may be ruined by a careless back-stroke. The file should cut in the direction of the set, as at *b* and *c*, Fig. 3. One or two strokes are usually sufficient to sharpen a tooth. The first, third, fifth, and so on, are filed first, then the saw is turned and the remainder filed. If the teeth are oblique, as in Fig. 4, then the direction of the file must be adjusted to fit this inclination, as shown by the arrows.

In the cross-cut, the file is held pointing upward and toward the handle of the saw, as shown by the arrows *a*, *a*, and *b*, *b*, Fig. 5. As this always leaves a wire-edge on each tooth, some prefer to file exactly in the opposite direction—that is, pointing downward and toward the point of the saw.

After filing, the saw should be *set*. For this important operation a good instrument must be used. Crude instruments, such as a block of wood, a nail punch, and a hammer, in the hands of an inexperienced workman, are more likely to ruin the saw than to benefit it. The teeth must be set with great regularity, in order to secure a smooth and straight cut. Morrill's instrument, shown in Figs. 6 and 7, acts by bending the point of the tooth with the punch *c*, the amount of the set being regulated by adjusting *a* and *b*.

Rip-saws, and also cross-cuts for fine work, should have very little set, and the points only of the teeth should be bent.

After setting the teeth, they should be finally trued, by rubbing the oil-stone lightly on the sides of the points.

Plate F.

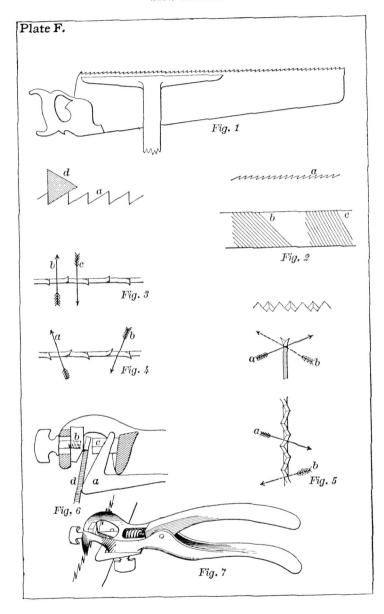

Fig. 1

Fig. 2

Fig. 3

Fig. 4

Fig. 5

Fig. 6

Fig. 7

Exercise 9.—Construction of a Half-Joint.

Material.—Stick of sawed pine, 3″ square and 4″ long.
Work.—To lay out and make a half-joint.

Plane the stick to exactly $2\frac{3}{4}''$ square, and mark the face-edge. Saw into two equal lengths after marking with the try-square and knife. When near the finish of the saw-cut, support the ends to prevent the stick from breaking, as shown at *a*, Fig. 1.

Set the marking-gauge to $1\frac{3}{8}''$; mark on the ends just cut and along the sides $2\frac{3}{4}''$, keeping the head of the gauge always on the face of the piece. These gauge-marks may be made without turning the pieces over, but allowing them to remain on the bench, face up, as shown in *a*, *a*, Fig. 2.

Now mark with the try-square and knife $2\frac{3}{4}''$ from the end, above the gauge-mark on one piece, and below the gauge-mark on the other, as at *b*, *b*, Fig. 2, always adjusting the handle of the try-square to the face of the stick.

The parts to be removed, shaded *a*, *a*, in Fig. 3, are now sawed out, using the rip-saw first and the cross-cut to finish. These parts, which are **waste** pieces, must contain the saw-kerfs, as shown in Fig. 3.

If the gauge and try-square have been properly adjusted to the face of the pieces, and the saw-kerfs accurately kept in the waste wood, the sticks will fit together, as shown in Fig. 4, so as to make the face even, or **flush**.

If the saws have not cut accurately, trim down carefully to the gauge and square-marks with the chisel.

Fig. 5 shows the pieces placed at right angles, in which position they should fit as well as in Fig. 4.

The same method of marking and cutting is employed to make the **scarf-joints**, of which Figs. 6, 7, and 8 are examples. In the joint (Fig. 8) the pieces are forced together by the key *a*, which is slightly wedge-shaped.

The joints (Figs. 9 and 10) used in building trusses may be made entirely with the saws, or with the saws and chisel. In practice, one piece of such joints is marked and cut first, laid in proper position on the other, which is then marked from the first.

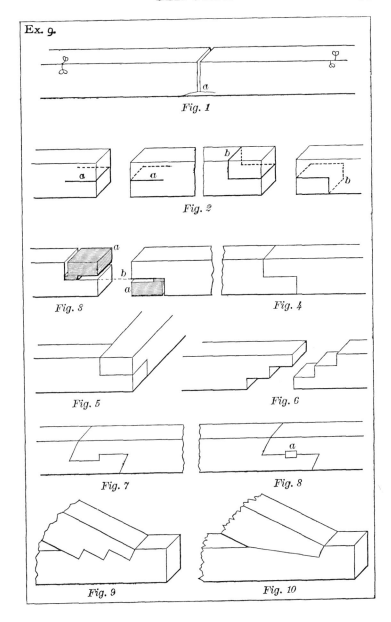

Ex. 9.

Fig. 1

Fig. 2

Fig. 3

Fig. 4

Fig. 5

Fig. 6

Fig. 7

Fig. 8

Fig. 9

Fig. 10

Exercise 10.—Modified Forms of the Half-Joint.

Fig. 1 shows the pieces in position and marked for a **lap-joint**, commonly used in building frame houses; Fig. 2, the upper piece cut to receive the vertical one. In nailing the pieces together, the vertical one is forced up against the **shoulder,** *a,* of the horizontal. This shoulder adds to the firmness of the joint, and the **rabbet** gives more secure nailing. The rabbet for timbers should have about the proportions shown in the figures.

Fig. 3 shows the ordinary rabbeted-joint of boards to be united by nailing. In laying out the rabbet, the mark *a,* Fig. 4, must be made with try-square and knife, the mark *b* with the marking-gauge; saw on the mark *a* with the cross-cut, and then chisel down the rabbet to the mark *b.* The horizontal piece may project slightly over the vertical, if it is intended to be finished with a plane.

Fig. 5 shows a **grooved** joint; the groove is marked with try-square and knife, the depth at the ends gauged. It is cut out with saw and chisel. This joint is used where there is apt to be a displacement sidewise, and also to make water-tight structures. In the latter case the groove is made a little narrower than the thickness of the tongue, which is slightly chamfered. The groove and tongue are then coated with white-lead and forced together.

Fig. 6 is a modified form of the grooved joint. Where there is not enough wood beyond the groove to give sufficient strength, the groove may be made smaller, usually half size. It is cut the same as that of Fig. 5, or with a rabbet-plane.

The difficulty of giving a good appearance to joints like Fig. 3 leads to various devices for finishing, the commonest of which is the **bead.** This is worked on the edge by a plane, the shape of which for cutting a $\frac{1}{4}''$ bead is shown in Fig. 8; the iron cuts only the depth *a,* and the round *b;* the portion *c* of the sole acts as a stop to regulate the depth, and *d* as a guide against the edge of the board. The form cut is shown at *a,* Fig. 9, and is called a single bead; by reversing the plane and cutting on the other side, a double bead is formed, as at *b,* Fig. 9.

Fig. 7 shows applications of the bead. Although either piece may be beaded, it is customary to bead the tongued edge of a board

Ex. 10.

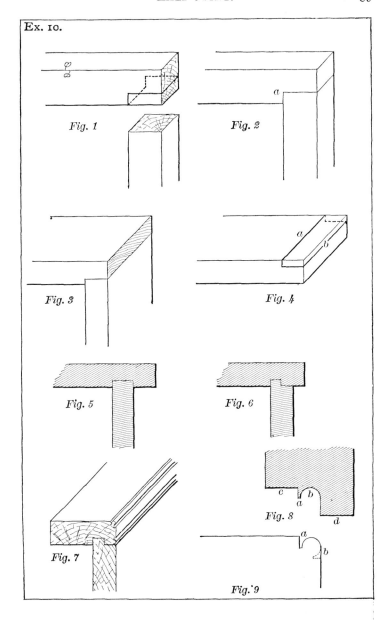

Fig. 1

Fig. 2

Fig. 3

Fig. 4

Fig. 5

Fig. 6

Fig. 7

Fig. 8

Fig. 9

Exercise 11.—Construction of a Mortise-Joint.

Materials.—The sticks of Exercise 9, after cutting off the half-joint.

Work.—To unite the pieces with a through mortise-joint.

Hold the pieces in the position shown in Fig. 1, with the faces toward you. The upper is to have a **tenon** formed on its end, and the lower a **mortise** cut into it.

Adjust the upper piece 2″ from the end of the lower; mark with a sharp pencil the width of the upper piece on the face-edge of the lower (*a, a*, Fig. 1). With these points as guides, mark with the try-square and pencil on three sides of the mortise-piece, as shown at *a, a*, Fig. 2; and with the try-square and knife, mark all around the tenon-piece $3\frac{1}{4}$″ from its end, as at *b, b*.

Set the gauge at $\frac{7}{8}$″, and mark on the end and sides of the tenon-piece, and on the top and bottom of the mortise-piece, as at *a, a*, Fig. 3. Then set the gauge at $1\frac{1}{8}$″ and mark between the same limits as before, producing the lines *b, b*, Fig. 4. Now place the tenon-piece on the mortise-piece, and note that the marks correspond exactly.

Saw the tenon, observing the instructions in Exercise 9, in regard to the saw-kerf and waste wood. In order to enter the mortise, the tenon (*a*, Fig. 5) must have its edges removed by chamfering, as at *b*; the measures, shown at *c*, Fig. 5, are marked with the pencil and rule, and the chamfer cut with the chisel.

To cut out the mortise, bore with the brace and $\frac{7}{8}$″ **center-bit** two holes in the mortise-piece, as at *a, a*, Fig. 6, about one half way through; then turn the piece over and bore down to meet the first holes. With the chisel and **mallet,** remove the part *b* between the holes, cutting first one side then the other with the edge of the chisel, parallel to the grain, *c*, and with the bevel side down, so as to throw out the chips. Next turn the chisel, and cut down the ends of the mortise as at *d*, leaving a margin of wood for finishing.

The mortise is now fitted for the tenon by cutting away the margin (*a, a*, Fig. 7) and paring the sides until the tenon passes snugly through. Test the sides of the mortise for flatness with the blade of the try-square.

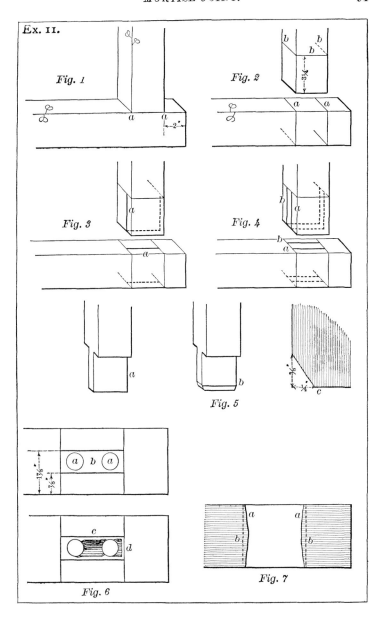

Fig. 1

Fig. 2

Fig. 3

Fig. 4

Fig. 5

Fig. 6

Fig. 7

Exercise 12.—Pinning the Mortise-Joint.

Material.—The joint of Exercise 11, and a piece of hard wood, $\frac{1}{4}''$ square and about 5″ long.

Work.—To fasten the tenon in the mortise with a pin.

Bore with a $\frac{5}{8}''$ **auger-bit,** through the face of the piece and mortise, 1″ below the face-edge, as shown in Fig. 1. The line *a* is marked by pencil and rule, and the point *b* marked in the middle of this line for starting the point of the bit. The hole is not bored all the way, but when the point shows through, as at *a*, Fig. 2, turn the piece around and bore from that side to complete the hole. By this means a clean cut is made on both sides of the piece. Test the auger-bit with the try-square, to keep it straight until fairly started into the wood.

Place the tenon in the mortise and mark the center of the hole on it with the point of the bit. Remove the tenon, and start the bit about $\frac{1}{16}''$ nearer the shoulder. The hole thus bored (Fig. 3) is not **in a line** with that of the mortise, as shown at *a*, Fig. 4, but when the pin is forced through, the pieces are brought closer together, forming a stiffer and stronger joint.

The pin is planed to $\frac{5}{8}''$ square, chamfered with plane or chisel to an octagonal shape, rounded and pointed with the chisel, as shown in Fig. 5, which is just one half size. In practice, the pin is driven in flush with the face of the mortise-piece, the protruding portion being either allowed to remain, or sawed off close.

For large through mortise-joints, such as are seen in the heavy frames of barns and mills, two oak pins are used, as at *a*, Fig. 6. Sometimes the pins are intended to act like wedges and force the parts together, as shown at *b*, Fig. 6. This joint is common in machine-frames.

Formerly, when pins were used to a greater extent, they were compressed by being forced through a tapering hole in an iron block. This had the effect of binding the pin firmly in the joint.

Fig. 7 is an example of a double mortise, and is used for securing the central leg of a table to the top. It is sometimes made without the shoulders *a*, *a*, which is bad practice, because they give greater stability to the joint.

Ex. 12.

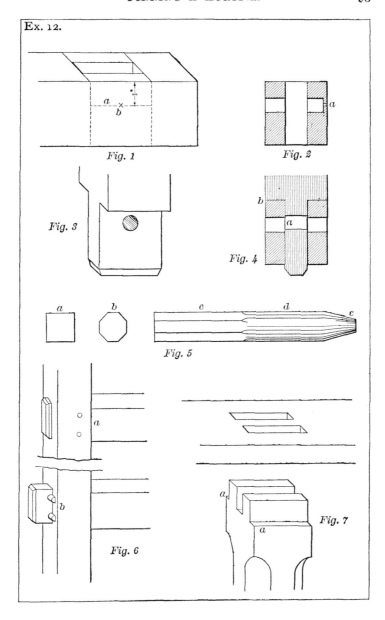

Fig. 1

Fig. 2

Fig. 3

Fig. 4

Fig. 5

Fig. 6

Fig. 7

Exercise 13.—Construction of a Stub-Mortise.

Material.—The same pieces as before, after removing the pinned joint.

Work.—To lay out, cut, and fasten a stub-mortise joint.

Use the same methods and measurements in marking as in Exercise 11, except that the tenon is to be $\frac{3}{4}''$ long, and the mortise $1''$ deep, and $1''$ from the end of the piece. Fig. 1 represents the work laid out, the lines *a, a,* marked with try-square and knife, and the lines *b, b,* with the marking-gauge. After cutting the tenon, a very small chamfer, about $\frac{1}{8}''$, may be cut on its end without marking.

The holes bored by the center-bit should not be more than $1''$ deep. When a large number of holes are to be bored the same depth, a wooden stop is made by boring a hole through a block of wood, so that the stem of the bit will pass through it, but of proper thickness to prevent the tool cutting beyond the required amount.

In removing chips from the mortise, do not pry with the chisel on the sides and ends. In testing the mortise, hold the chisel against the side, and note whether it is square or inclined. The mortise and tenon should fit very snugly.

With the tenon in place, bore with a $\frac{1}{2}''$ auger-bit a hole through the bottom of the mortise-piece, and into the middle of the tenon-piece about $3''$, as shown in Fig. 3. This is to receive an iron **bolt.** At $1\frac{1}{2}''$ from the shoulder, and on the inside of the tenon-piece (*a,* Fig. 3), cut with chisels a hole large enough to receive the **nut** (*b,* Fig. 3) of the bolt. The **head,** *d,* of the bolt should have a **washer,** *c,* to prevent it crushing the wood. In some cases it is necessary to **sink** the head flush with the surface, as at *a,* Fig. 4.

The stub-mortise is extensively used in heavy machine-frames.

Fig. 5 shows a **blind-mortise,** used in making furniture. Sometimes the end of the tenon is spread with wedges, as at *a, b,* Fig. 6.

Fig. 7 shows a form of stub-mortise used in heavy railroad-trestles. The timbers are secured by iron straps spiked to the sides.

Fig. 8 is a form of joint used in trusses, the broken line *a* showing the shape of the tenon.

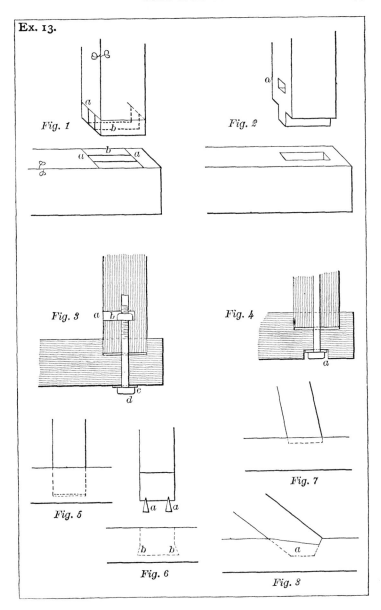

Ex. 13.

Fig. 1

Fig. 2

Fig. 3

Fig. 4

Fig. 5

Fig. 6

Fig. 7

Fig. 8

Exercise 14.—Construction of a Dovetail-Joint.

Material.—Same pieces as before, with stub-mortise sawed off.
Work.—To lay out and construct an end-dovetail-joint.

Wherever oblique cuts are to be made, great care is necessary in marking.

Place the pieces in the position shown in Fig. 1; the upper piece is to have the tenon, or **dovetail**, the lower the mortise. With try-square and sharp pencil, mark lines around three sides of each piece, at a distance from the end equal to the width of the opposite piece, as shown at a, a, Fig. 1. These pencil-marks should be very light, so as to be easily cleaned off with sand-paper or smoothing-plane.

The measurements of the dovetail are given in Fig. 3. Set the gauge at $\frac{3}{8}''$, and mark the lines b, b, Fig. 1. Set it at $2\frac{3}{8}''$, and mark the lines b', b'. Set it at $\frac{1}{4}''$, and mark the line c, and press the point only of the gauge at d, d. Set the gauge at $1\frac{1}{4}''$, and mark the line c', and the points e, e. Bring the edge of the blade of the try-square to coincide with the lines b and c on the end of the mortise-piece, and mark with the knife a line joining them. Do the same for all the oblique lines, as shown in Fig. 1.

The tenon (a, Fig. 2) is sawed out, and the sides of the mortise b also cut with the saw. The mortise is finished with the chisel, used as shown in Fig. 4. A vertical cut is made as at a, using the mallet, then one at b; these to be repeated until one half through the piece, then cut on the opposite side. Avoid cutting into the sides of the mortise by inclining the chisel. The same caution must be observed in keeping some of the wood at c, Fig. 4, until the last, when it is carefully cut away, and the surface tested with the try-square. The sides of the mortise usually need a little paring before the tenon will fit. This done, the pieces should go together easily, but without **play** or **open** joints, and appear as in Fig. 5.

Fig. 6 shows an oblique dovetail-joint used in a gallows-brace, which is made of lighter material than the rest of the frame, let in about one half its thickness and pinned as shown in the figure. In practice the oblique marks on the brace are obtained directly from the beams, the dovetails are then cut, and the mortises marked on the beams from them.

Ex. 14.

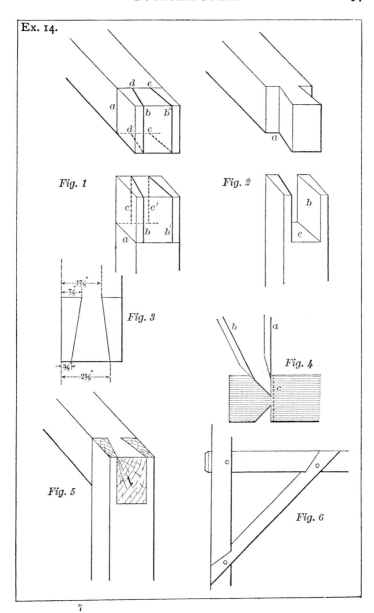

Fig. 1

Fig. 2

Fig. 3

Fig. 4

Fig. 5

Fig. 6

Exercise 15.—Construction of a Miter-Joint.

Material.—A strip of pine, $2\frac{1}{2}''$ wide, $\frac{1}{2}''$ thick, and about $16''$ long.
Work.—To make a miter-joint.

Mark with the try-square and knife two lines across the middle of the strip from a and e, Fig. 1, about $\frac{1}{2}''$ apart. Measure carefully the length $a\,b$, and lay it off on the face-edge, to obtain $a\,c$, then mark with the knife and blade of the try-square, $c\,b$. Do the same on the opposite side for the mark $f\,d$. From c and d mark lines on the $\frac{1}{2}''$ side square with the face-edge.

Saw very accurately against the lines $c\,b$ and $d\,f$, the waste wood being toward a in each case. The pieces put together as in Fig. 2, and the try-square, indicated at a, applied to them, should show a true miter-joint.

The joint may not be true, and, to determine which side is at fault, adjust the **T-bevel** to exactly $45°$, the value of a true miter. To do this, repeat the operation shown in Fig. 1, but more carefully. With a sharp pencil mark on a board with a straight-edge the line $a\,c$, Fig, 3, against the try-square; turn the square over, and test the line by marking another on it; if these separate, make a line exactly between the two—this should be correct; then measure off accurate equal lengths $a\,c$ and $a\,b$; join the points c and b; adjust the T-bevel to this last line, as in the figure, and test the pieces with it.

Two faults are shown in Figs. 4 and 5, and the broken lines indicate the wood to be removed in order to correct them, which may be done with the chisel, saw, or plane.

To correct with the saw, fasten the true side with the hand-screw, as shown at a, Fig. 6, square to the stop of the bench-hook, press the piece b against the stop and the piece a; saw between the pieces, so as to cut on b, while a guides the saw.

To correct with the plane the piece is held as shown in Fig. 7, the iron cutting that part which is to be removed. This maintains a square end as well as correcting the bevel.

If a thick piece, fasten in the vise, and with a sharp fine-set smoothing-plane, make very short strokes, as indicated by the arrows at a, b, and c, Fig. 8, cutting only those places where wood should be removed.

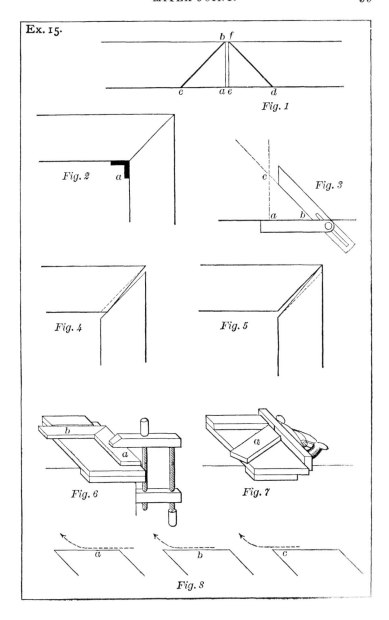

Ex. 15.

Fig. 1

Fig. 2

Fig. 3

Fig. 4

Fig. 5

Fig. 6

Fig. 7

Fig. 8

Exercise 16.—Use of the Miter-Box.

Material.—A piece of molding, 18″ long and 2″ wide.

Work.—To saw the molding in the miter-box and test the result by
uniting the pieces.

The successive cuts of the molding are shown in Fig. 4, starting from the right-hand end. Adjust each cut carefully, so that
no portion of the edges remains between the cuts. In pushing
the saw, which in ordinary practice is a back-saw or small thin
cross-cut, guide it so as not to injure the saw-kerfs of the miter-
box, and use very little force. The molding cut as directed gives
two sets of four pieces. Each set may be fastened to a thin board
4″ square, with small finishing nails, as in Fig. 5.

In molding a frame or panel, the lengths are accurately measured, usually by laying the molding on the side of the frame, and
marking on its edge with a knife. The inside measurement of the
frame (*a b*, Fig. 6) gives marks as at *b* and *d*, Fig. 3, which are adjusted to the saw-kerfs on the side *d*, Fig. 1, of the miter-box. The
outside measurement (*c d*, Fig. 6) gives marks as at *a* and *c*, Fig. 3,
and these are adjusted to the kerfs on the bottom piece of the box,
as at *f*, Fig. 1. But in the lower moldings, shown in Fig. 6, the
marks are made in the rabbets, and a little care must be taken to
adjust them to the kerfs on the bottom of the miter-box.

Very large moldings are built up of several elements fastened
to frames, as in Fig. 7. Fig. 8 shows a joint commonly used in
trimming windows and doors, in which only the molded part is
mitered. This miter is cut with the chisel alone, or with the aid
of a guide, as shown at *a*, Fig. 9.

A **miter-box** for ordinary work should be about 18″ long, and
made of hard wood, 4″ wide and 1½″ thick. The middle or bottom piece (*a*, Fig. 1) must be planed perfectly flat and with parallel and square edges; the sides (*b, c*, Fig. 1) firmly fastened
with screws. The holes for these screws should be bored as shown
in Fig. 2; the first boring, *b*, should admit the smooth shaft of
the screw *a*; the second boring, *c*, should be smaller and the full
length of the screw; the top of the hole, *d*, is countersunk for the
head of the screw. The saw-cuts are laid out from the face-edge
(*d*, Fig. 1), and made with the saw which is to be used in the box.

Ex. 16.

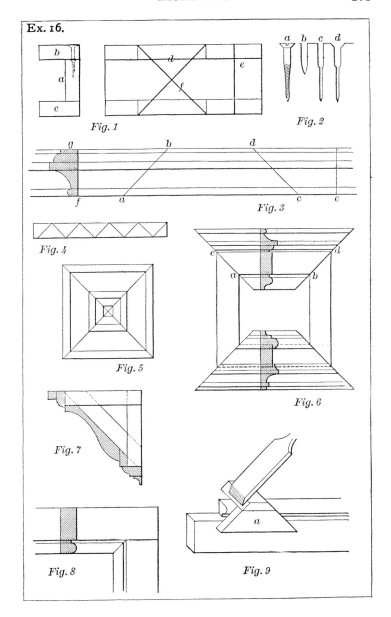

Fig. 1

Fig. 2

Fig. 3

Fig. 4

Fig. 5

Fig. 6

Fig. 7

Fig. 8

Fig. 9

Exercise 17.—Construction of a Stretcher–Joint.

Material.—Pine, 2″ wide, ¾″ thick, and 12″ long.
Work.—To make a joint such as that used in frames for stretching canvas.

This joint is a combination of miter and half joint, and is laid out as shown in Fig. 1. The miter is on the face-side, and ¼″ thick, the tenon also ¼″ thick. For the miter the gauge is set at ¼″, but for the tenon at ½″. To avoid mistakes, the parts to be cut out should be shaded as in Fig. 2. Saw the tenon and mortise with a back-saw before sawing the miter.

With an ⅛″ chisel, or better, an ⅛″ float (Fig. 5, Plate B), cut the grooves for wedges as shown in Fig. 4. The groove for the horizontal one is made in the tenon-piece, close up to the tenon, and, for the vertical one, in the mortise. Make the wedges of hard wood, with the grain parallel to one side, which must be in contact with the end wood of the pieces as they are driven in.

The pine piece for this exercise may be sawed out of a ½″ board. This board should rest on carpenter's horses; the rip-saw is used first, the kerf is made on the pencil-mark, is brought just up to the cross-mark, and finished with a vertical stroke. In marking, an allowance of about ⅛″ should be made for planing and finishing.

Fig. 5 shows a form of stretcher-joint sometimes seen in picture-frames. This joint will stretch the canvas fairly well, but has not the control over wrinkles as that of Fig. 4 has.

Fig. 6 shows a form of miter-joint in which oblique saw-kerfs are made for the insertion of thin pieces of hard wood. The joint has somewhat the character of a dovetail, and should be well glued.

A miter-joint in thin pieces is usually secured by a veneer, glued in as in Fig. 7. The pieces are first mitered, then fastened in the jaws of a hand-screw or bench-vise, and the saw-cut made for the insertion of the veneer.

Picture-frames are generally made by mitering, gluing, and fastening with small finishing-nails at the outer corners. Occasionally we see frames with joints like those of Fig. 3, and sometimes with two tenons and mortises instead of one. Since glue holds better on side-wood than on end-wood, the latter are much stronger.

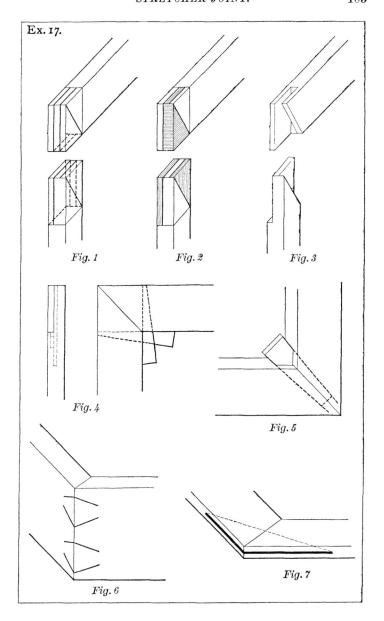

Ex. 17.

Fig. 1   Fig. 2   Fig. 3

Fig. 4

Fig. 5

Fig. 6

Fig. 7

Exercise 18.—Uniting with Dowels.

Material.—Two blocks of wood, about 3″ wide, 2″ thick, and 4″ to 5″ long.

Work.—To mark for the positions of the dowels, and join the pieces.

Plane the surfaces of the blocks until perfectly flat, test them by bringing the surfaces in contact, and note whether they touch all around. The dowel-joint is a weak one, and, unless the surfaces are flat and brought in close contact, the dowels will be of no service in holding the pieces together.

Select positions for the dowels on the pieces to be united, so that other joints or cuts will not interfere with them. Fix a point (*a*, Fig. 1) on each piece, at corresponding distances from the edges, for one dowel. With this first point for a center, mark the arcs *b, b* with the compasses, and mark on them corresponding points for the second dowel. From the points *a, a* describe the arcs *c, c ;* and from *b, b* the arcs *d, d*, crossing *c, c* to give the places for the third dowels. With a ⅜″ auger or **dowel-bit** bore a hole about 1″ deep at each point. Saw three dowels from a dowel-rod, about 2″ long, and slightly chamfer their ends with the chisel or rasp. Drive them into one piece. Measure the depths of the holes in the other piece, see that the dowels are not too long, and then force the pieces together.

An ordinary way of getting the marks for the dowels is to place small shot in position on one piece and press the other piece on them.

Fig. 2 shows a method of marking with try-square and gauge for dowels ; Fig. 3, the dowels in position and the pieces ready for gluing.

When dowel-rods can not be obtained, the dowels may be made with a dowel-plate. Fig. 4, *a*, is a dowel-plate, of iron or steel, and having a number of holes of different sizes in it, through which rough pieces of wood, *b*, are forced with the hammer.

Fig. 5 shows the diagonal positions of dowels in uniting thick pieces. Fig. 6 illustrates the use of dowels in holding the parts of a core-box in position. Fig. 7 illustrates the use of dowels in uniting the parts of a hand-rail; *a* is a square nut, *b* a nut (shown enlarged at *c*) with projections, so that it may be turned with a punch.

Ex. 18.

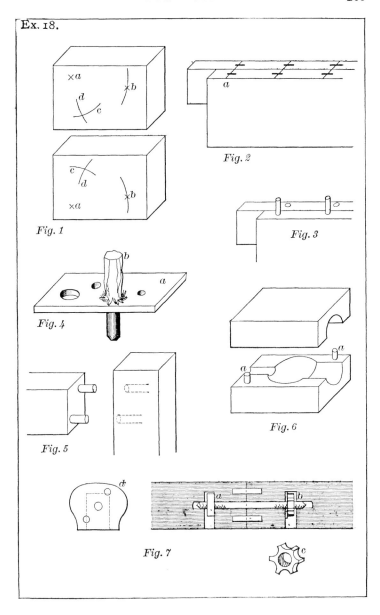

Fig. 1

Fig. 2

Fig. 3

Fig. 4

Fig. 5

Fig. 6

Fig. 7

Exercise 19.—Gluing.

Material.—Two blocks of wood.

Glue prepared for use.

Work.—To face the blocks and unite them with glue.

To prepare glue: Fill the inner vessel of the **glue-pot** about one third full of dried glue; cover with cold water and set aside for several hours; after which keep the outer vessel about one half full of water, and boil with the inner vessel in place. Add enough hot water to the melted glue until the drip from the brush begins to form drops.

Plane the surfaces of the blocks perfectly flat. Test them by holding together as in Fig. 1, and note if the surfaces come together at the edges, and particularly at opposite corners, as *a* and *c*. Mark the edges of the block, so that you will know which way they go together. The surfaces may be roughened with the **scratch-plane**, and must not be oily. Adjust the **hand-screws** a little wider apart than the thickness of the united blocks.

Heat the blocks and apply the hot glue to both surfaces, then rub them together, forcing out the excess of glue. Rest the lower jaw of the hand-screw on the bench, and place the blocks well into the screws, as shown in Fig. 2; tighten the screw *a* until a slight pressure is exerted on *c, c*, Fig. 2; then turn the screw *b* until the jaws close down at *d, d*, Fig. 3. Examine carefully to see that the joint is evenly closed, adjusting the pieces with the hammer, if not in place. Remove the excess of glue with a wet sponge, or with the chisel when partially set, after which stand the pieces aside for several hours.

In gluing together the edges of boards, or the parts of a door, **clamps** must be used, as shown in Fig. 4.

Fig. 5 represents a block built up by uniting several pieces; the pieces *b, b* may be doweled as well as glued, the pieces *a, a* simply glued. Where glue alone is used, some attention should be paid to the direction and character of the grain. If possible, the grain should be parallel and alike in size. A coarse grain, *a*, will not unite well with a fine grain, *b*, Fig. 6, especially if the pieces are not perfectly seasoned. Fig. 7 illustrates a way in which large pieces are built up in pattern-work.

Ex. 19.

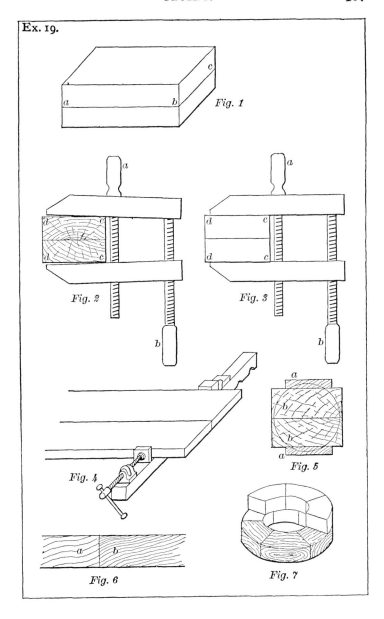

Fig. 1

Fig. 2

Fig. 3

Fig. 4

Fig. 5

Fig. 6

Fig. 7

Exercise 20.—Examples of Glued Joints.

Fig. 1 shows the usual way in which furniture is joined—that is, with dowels and glue. While there are many joints in furniture and cabinet-work for which the dowel is especially suited, there are also many joints in which it is constantly used, but not at all suited, and where a well-made mortised joint would be much stronger.

Fig. 2 shows a blind-mortise-joint used in well-made cabinet work. The tenon of such a joint should have shoulders on at least three sides. Glue the mortise and tenon, and not the shoulder.

Fig. 3 shows the manner of stiffening a joint, by means of **angle-pieces** (*a, a*). These are carefully fitted, glued, and rubbed until the glue sets.

As another example of angle-pieces we have that shown in Fig. 4, in which the pieces *a, a, a,* stiffen the joint by acting like braces between the boards. This practice is very extensive in the manufacture of furniture, and is also used between the tread and riser of a stair. Where greater strength is required, and the exposed surfaces of the work are to be kept as free as possible from marks, as in fastening a table-top to its frame, the pieces may be screwed together as shown in Fig. 5. The recesses are first cut with a gouge or one of the recent forms of bits shown in Fig. 6 ; then the holes are made for the screws, which are usually short and thick. This new form of bit is guided by a sharp rim, *a,* which prepares the way for the cutter, *b,* and may be started against the side of a board for an oblique cut, as in Fig. 5, as well as a straight boring.

It frequently happens that where boards have to be securely united, screws must be used through a surface which is afterward to be finished. Fig. 7 shows the boards prepared for the screws ; the space *a* is cut very neatly, and afterward filled with a round piece of wood corresponding in color and direction of grain. Fig. 8 shows the pieces screwed together, and the round block, *b,* glued in place, after which the surface is planed. The round piece may be pared with the chisel, or turned in a lathe.

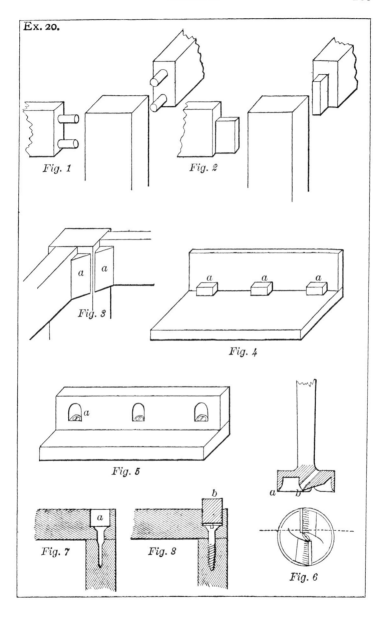

Ex. 20.

Fig. 1

Fig. 2

Fig. 3

Fig. 4

Fig. 5

Fig. 6

Fig. 7

Fig. 8

Exercise 21.—Laying out a Dovetailed Box.

Material.—Dressed pine-board, 14″ wide and ⅝″ thick.

Work.—1. Saw off 17″ of the board.

    2. Lay out the parts of the box on the board.

    3. Saw and plane the pieces to proper size.

The dimensions of the box are: length 8″, height $4\frac{1}{2}$″, width 5″, thickness of material ⅝″, depth of inside $3\frac{1}{4}$″, as in Fig. 1.

It will take 17″ in length of a board 14″ wide to furnish enough material. Saw this from the board, resting on horses, after marking with the large pencil and steel square, and allowing for wind-checks, if at the end.

The 17″ piece must now be carefully examined on both sides for checks, shakes, knots, sap-wood, resin-pockets, and other imperfections, and the box laid out so that these faults may come in the waste wood. If the wood is clear, the pieces may be laid out as shown in Fig. 2: *a*, the top; *b*, bottom; *c, c*, front and back; *d, d*, ends; *e, e*, waste wood to make up for any defects that may occur. Notice that all the pieces are laid out larger than the true size. Thus the top and bottom are $8\frac{1}{2}$″ by $5\frac{1}{2}$″, the front and back $8\frac{1}{2}$″ by $3\frac{1}{2}$″, and the ends $5\frac{1}{2}$″ by $3\frac{1}{2}$″. This is allowed for working margins.

If a 9″ board is used, the pieces may be obtained with less waste, as shown in Fig. 3. It would take $22\frac{1}{2}$″ length to provide the material.

In sawing out the pieces where they are short, as in this case, those of the same kind should be kept together until after planing; *a* with *b*, *c* with *c*, and *d* with *d*, Fig. 2. The pieces are first squared on one edge, which becomes the face-edge; from this the opposite edge is gauged and planed.

The top and bottom may be put aside without planing until the other pieces are glued together.

Plane to $3\frac{1}{4}$″ wide, carefully measure and mark with the knife the length, 8″, of the front and back pieces, and saw accurately with the back-saw.

It is sometimes the practice, after sawing the pieces apart, to adjust the cut ends and face-edges together, and make one knife-mark across the edges, thus securing equal lengths.

Ex. 21.

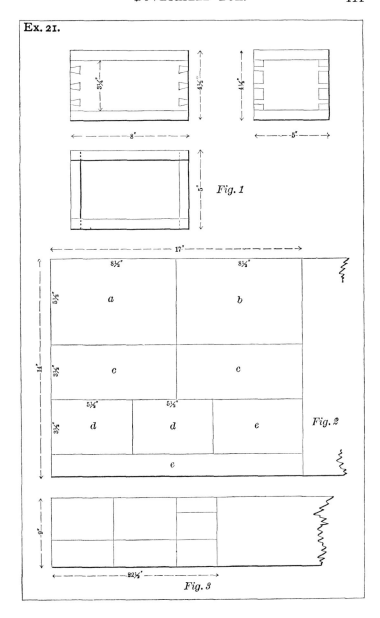

Fig. 1

Fig. 2

Fig. 3

Exercise 22.—Laying out and cutting the Dovetails.

Material.—Front and back pieces of the dovetailed box.
Work.—Marking and cutting the mortises.

The pieces are marked with a sharp pencil on both sides and edge ⅜″ from the ends, as at *a, a, b, b,* Fig. 1. Or the pieces are brought together and points marked on both at the face-edge, by which the lines *a, b,* Fig. 1, are squared. It is very necessary to square the lines from the face-edge, otherwise the joints are likely to be open on one side or the other.

On these lines mark the places for the dovetails as indicated in Fig. 2. This may be done in either of two ways: the measure may be carefully made on a cardboard and transferred from it to each of the lines with a sharp point; or the marking-gauge may be set at each measure and its point used to mark the distance on the lines.

In Fig. 2, one end is shown full size with the measures; on the line from *a* to *b* each space has its value; while from *c* to *d* each point is measured from the face-edge, and any inaccuracy given to one of the points is not continued along the line. This latter method is truer, but more difficult. Having marked the points, the slanting sides of the joints are marked with the knife along the T-bevel set to a certain angle. This angle, an arbitrary one, is shown in Fig. 3. On a board with a true edge measure ⅜″, *b, c*; from *b* draw the line *a b* with try-square; lay off on this line a point 3″ from *b*; join this last point and *c*; adjust the T-bevel to this line, *a c*. The bevel is applied to the ends of the pieces in marking the lines *g, g,* and *i, i,* and the marks across the ends *h, h,* completed with the try-square and knife.

In cutting out the mortises, it would be well to shade the parts to be removed, then saw, observing the rule in regard to the saw-kerf, as in Fig. 4. The pieces are cut out as directed in Exercise 14. In finishing the cuts, use a small chisel grasped by the right hand resting on the piece (Fig. 5), so that the hand acts both as a power and a guide or check to prevent the tool cutting beyond half the depth. The cut should be as near as possible straight across, but rather hollow than round, as at *d,* Fig. 6. In testing use a small steel square (Fig. 8, Plate A).

Ex. 22.

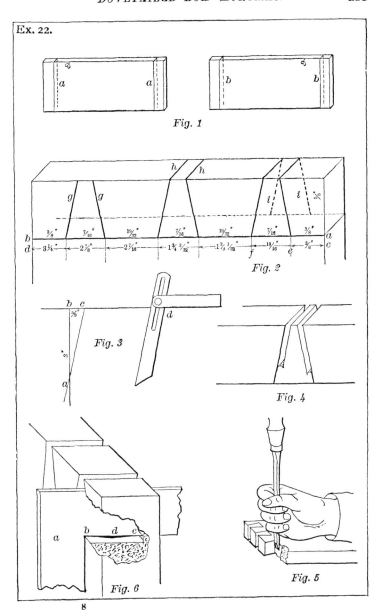

Fig. 1

Fig. 2

Fig. 3

Fig. 4

Fig. 5

Fig. 6

8

Exercise 23.—Marking and cutting the Tenons.

Material.—The end pieces of the dovetailed box.
Work.—1. Marking and cutting the tenons.
    2. Gluing together the sides.

Mark with a sharp pencil $\frac{3}{8}''$ from the ends all around the end pieces. Stand the front, back, and end pieces on the bench in the positions which they will have when the box is completed. Mark the outer and upper corners of adjoining parts with the same sign or number.

Fasten the end piece numbered *1* in the vise, with its number up and out; place the front piece on the end piece as shown in Fig. 1, resting the back part on a plane-stock or block of wood. Adjust the two pieces with the try-square, its handle against the face-edge of the front piece, and its blade up against the end piece. Hold the upper piece in this adjusted position, while with a knife or point you mark along the sides of the mortise on the top of the end piece. The marks should appear like those of *a*, Fig. 2. Mark the other ends in the same way. With try-square and knife mark from the ends of the lines *a*, Fig. 2, down to the pencil-mark, as at *b* and *c*.

Saw with the back-saw as shown in Fig. 3, keeping the kerf in the waste wood.

Saw the corner waste pieces, and chisel out the middle ones, making the surfaces *a*, *a*, Fig. 4, as flat as possible. Carefully fit the corresponding parts, using the chisel for paring where neccessary.

With a sharp finely set smoothing-plane clean off the inside surfaces of the pieces. Open two hand-screws ready for use in the positions shown in Fig. 5.

The pieces are now warmed, the tenons and mortices glued, the parts pressed together and placed in the hand-screws, which are tightened sufficiently to close the joints but not bend in the sides. The gluing process should be performed quickly, and the student should have a fellow-student assist him.

Clean off as much excess glue as possible, wiping the inside with a wet sponge or cloth, and set aside the box for several hours.

Ex. 23.

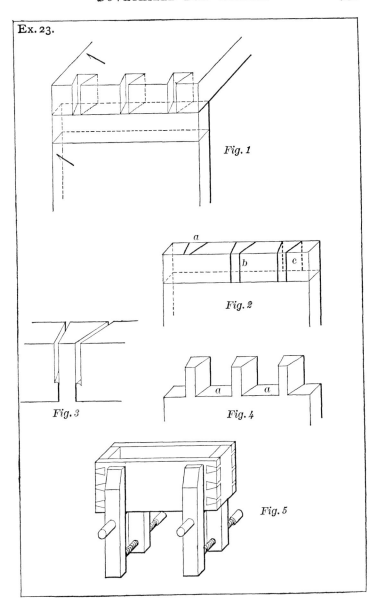

Fig. 1

Fig. 2

Fig. 3

Fig. 4

Fig. 5

Exercise 24.—Finishing the Box.

Work.—1. Examine and prepare the smoothing-plane for finishing.
  2. Smooth and plane flat the bottom edge of the sides, and glue on
      the bottom piece.
  3. Smooth the joints and sides.

Remove and sharpen the iron of the smoothing-plane. Examine the sole of the plane with the try-square for flatness. The fault in wooden planes, particularly if new, is shown in Fig. 1; holding the blade on the sole, you will notice that the wood just behind the throat is too high, as at *b*. This is caused by unequal shrinkage of the wood when the iron and wedge are in place, and must be remedied by planing down the sole with a true, sharp, fine-set fore-plane or smoothing-plane. Unless the sole of the plane is perfectly flat, no good work can be performed with it.

Fig. 2 represents a **block-plane,** made of iron, with levers for adjusting its iron, and a movable toe-piece to regulate the opening of the throat. The iron, *c*, has its bevel side up, and is inclined about 20°. There is more friction with an iron plane, but it gives better results across the grain or on hard wood.

Fasten the box in the vise with the bottom upward; hold the plane in the position shown in *a*, Fig. 3; push it slowly along the side, to cut rather on the inside than outside of the pieces; turn the corners as shown by the arrow at *e*, Fig. 3. The tendency is to cut too much on the outer edge and on the corners, which must be carefully avoided. In all finishing the shavings must be very thin. After planing and testing the bottom for flatness, smooth the face of the bottom piece, glue it to the box, clean off the excess glue, and set aside for the glue to harden; after which, fasten the box in the vise with an end upward, and **clean off** the wood. Here the greatest care must be taken to prevent splitting off pieces in the manner shown in Fig. 4. In Fig. 5 the broken line shows the direction which the cutting edge should take, always raising the plane when nearly across. Plane from the edges toward the middle, and, if the middle becomes high, confine the strokes to the high part.

In framed work, as in Fig. 6, plane *a* and *b* first, then *c* and *d*, noting the direction of the grain, so as to secure a smooth surface.

Ex. 24.

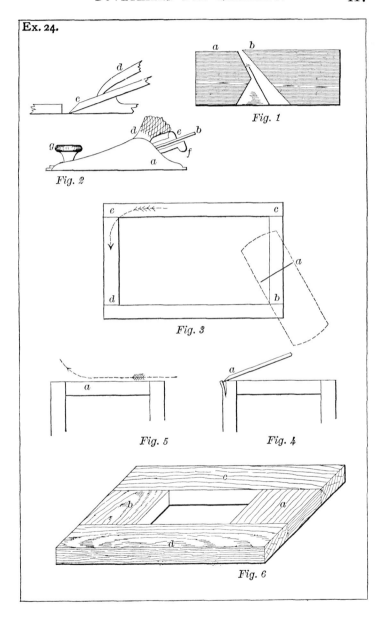

Fig. 1

Fig. 2

Fig. 3

Fig. 5

Fig. 4

Fig. 6

Exercise 25.—Hinging the Top to the Box.

Material.—1″ *middle*-size wrought-brass butts, ⅜″ brass screws to fit.
Work.—1. Prepare the upper edge of the box for the top.
    2. Smooth the top piece and square its back edge.
    3. Fit and fasten the hinges.
    4. Finish the edges of the top piece.

The hinges may have either of the three positions shown in Figs. 1, 2, and 3. For that of Fig. 3, **narrow**-size butts should be used, and the edges of the back piece and top chamfered, as at *a* and *b*.

Hold the hinge on the back piece ¾″ from the corner, and mark with the knife (*a*, *a*, Fig. 4). Repeat for the other hinge at the other end. Set the gauge, using the hinge for the distance (*c*, Fig. 1), and mark the lines (*b*, Fig. 4). Set the gauge, exactly one half the thickness of the hinge (*d*, Fig. 1), and mark the lines (*c*, Fig. 4). Hold the hinge so that it coincides with the marks *a*, *a*, and *b*, Fig. 4, and extend the lines *a*, *a*, up to *b* with the knife.

Cut down on the line *d*, Fig. 5, with the knife about the depth required; with the chisel cut out the corners, as shown at *a*, *a*, Fig. 5; and with the chisel in the position *c*, Fig. 5, make several cuts to finish the recess for the hinge. Place the hinge in the recess; with a **brad-awl** make holes smaller and not as deep as the length of the screw, and fasten the hinge with the screws. Repeat the cutting and fasten the other hinge. Close the butts, and place the top in position, resting on them; mark with the knife points on the top to correspond with the marks *a*, *a*, Fig. 4. From these marks as guides repeat the marking and cutting as for the back piece.

Screw the butts to the top, using one screw for each; then test the top by closing it, and remedy any defect by cutting or placing strips of cardboard under the butts, if cut away too much. Then put in the other screws. Finish the edges of the top piece, using the box as a guide. Smooth the face of the top.

The top may be secured with a brass hook and eye. Screw the eye in the middle of the front edge of the top; place the hook in the eye to determine the place for the screw.

Fig. 6 shows a table-hinge, and Fig. 7 a door-hinge.

Ex. 25.

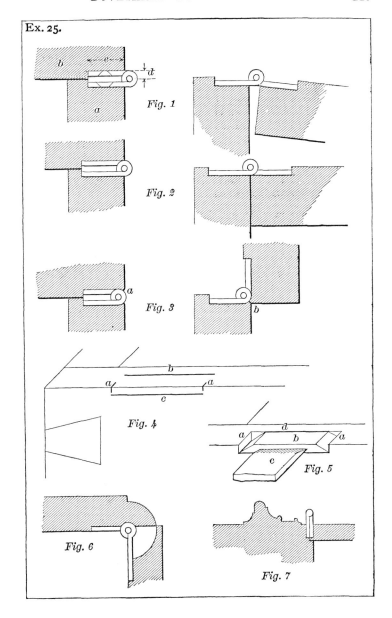

Fig. 1

Fig. 2

Fig. 3

Fig. 4

Fig. 5

Fig. 6

Fig. 7

Exercise 26.—Construction of a Drawer.

Material.—One piece of ash, to work 4″ wide, $\frac{7}{8}$″ thick, and $9\frac{1}{2}$″ long.
    Two pieces of maple, to work 4″ wide, $\frac{5}{8}$″ thick, and $14\frac{3}{4}$″ long.
    One piece of maple, to work $3\frac{5}{8}$″ wide, $\frac{1}{2}$″ thick, and $8\frac{1}{2}$″ long.
    One piece of whitewood, to work 14″ wide, $\frac{1}{2}$″ thick, and $8\frac{3}{4}$″ long.
Work.—1. Plane the pieces to the proper dimensions.
    2. Cut the dovetails on the front piece.
    3. Cut the mortises and grooves for the back piece in the sides.
    4. Plow the grooves in the front and sides for the bottom.
    5. Fit the back piece.
    6. Glue and nail the front sides and back together.
    7. Fit and place the bottom in position.

The pieces may be cut from boards, allowance being made for working, so as to produce a drawer of the dimensions given in Fig. 1.

In marking for the dovetails in the ash front, use the measures given in *a*, Fig. 2. In cutting out the dovetails, use the back-saw, as shown in Fig. 4. Chisel out the waste wood, being careful not to undercut the spaces, which should be frequently tested for squareness.

The mortises (shown at *c* and *d*, Fig. 2) are marked from the tenons. The grooves for the back are sawed and chiseled out $\frac{1}{8}$″ deep, $\frac{1}{2}$″ wide, and about $\frac{3}{4}$″ from the ends.

Place the $\frac{1}{4}$″ iron in the plow (*a*, Fig. 3), adjust it for a fine cut; set the bridge *b* so that the iron is $\frac{3}{8}$″ from it; set the stop *c* so that the iron will plow to a depth of $\frac{1}{4}$″; and first try the plow on some waste block before grooving the pieces.

The dovetail-joints are glued. The back piece is nailed with $1\frac{1}{4}$″ finishing or wire nails, which should be driven a short way below the surface with a nail-punch.

After the glue has hardened, the bottom is fitted and pushed in place. The edge of the bottom is marked with the gauge set at a little less than $\frac{1}{4}$″, and beveled with the jack-plane to about 1″ back from the edge.

The entire drawer is now finished with the smoothing-plane, and may be furnished with handle or lock. A lock is fitted somewhat like a hinge, the key-hole being the guide for its position.

Ex. 26.

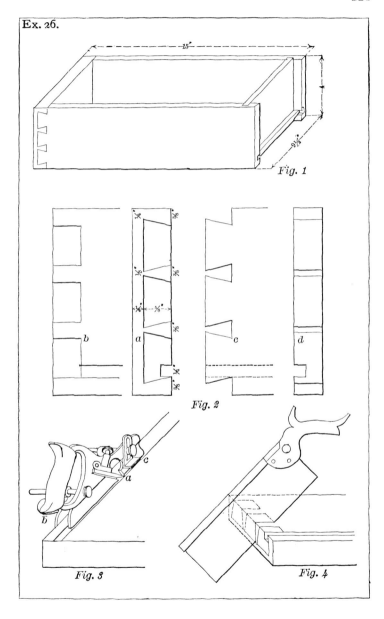

Fig. 1

Fig. 2

Fig. 3

Fig. 4

Exercise 27.—Construction of a Blind-Dovetailed Box.

Material.—$\frac{1}{2}''$ dressed mahogany.

Work.—To construct a box 9″ long, 6″ wide, and about 4″ high, with
    hidden joints.

The box will consist of two portions, the lower or box proper,
and a $1\frac{1}{4}''$ lid. To secure perfect coincidence between lid and box,
these are built together, and, after the box has been glued up, are
separated with the saw. An allowance from $\frac{1}{8}''$ to $\frac{3}{16}''$ must therefore be made for the saw-cut and finishing. The joints between
the sides are dovetailed with a mitered edge. The top is grooved
and mitered to the sides, and the bottom tongued, to fit a groove
in the sides.

Fig. 1, *a*, shows the details, drawn one half size of the end
piece, *c* a perspective of the same, *b* a perspective of the adjoining
piece. At *d, d, d*, is shown the separation to form the lid.

Fig. 2 gives the full-size details of the joint for the top and
also for the sides of the lid. The groove and miter are worked
with the plow and plane all around the top.

Fig 3 gives the details, also full size, for the bottom.

The dovetails are $\frac{3}{8}''$ long, and the mitered edge $\frac{1}{8}''$. At the
top, bottom, and adjoining the line of separation (*d*, Fig. 1) of the
sides, the joints are mitered, as shown in *b* and *c*, Fig. 1.

In working the joints, cut all the grooves and rabbets first,
then the dovetails, and lastly the mitered surfaces. On the ends
of the sides, saw and chisel a rabbet $\frac{1}{4}''$ wide and $\frac{3}{8}''$ deep; mark
out the dovetails; saw both tenons and mortises, as shown in Fig.
4, Example 26; chisel out and fit the dovetails and miters.

To make the joint between the lid and box dust-tight, strips
$\frac{1}{8}''$ thick and $\frac{3}{4}''$ wide may be glued around the inside of the box,
projecting above its edge about $\frac{3}{16}''$, and with mitered joints. The
projecting edge should be round.

Or a **tray** about $1\frac{1}{4}''$ deep may be made of thin material, to rest
on an inside lining about $\frac{3}{16}''$ thick and $1\frac{1}{4}''$ high.

In Fig. 4 the mitered edge is shown rounded, as frequently seen
in cabinet-work. Fig. 5 is a simpler joint than the above. Sometimes the corners are left open to be afterward filled with a narrow
strip of some fancy wood.

Ex. 27.

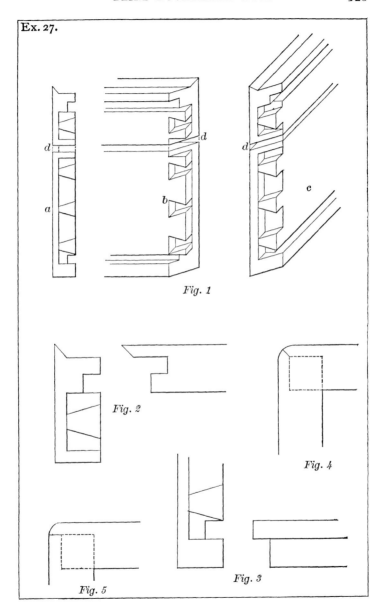

Fig. 1

Fig. 2

Fig. 4

Fig. 3

Fig. 5

Exercise 28.—Framing.

In the eight exercises following, the actual sizes will be given, from which the student will calculate the proportionate measures for his models.

Fig. 1 represents a portion of the frame of a wooden house. The **sills,** a, are 3″ by 6″, with half-joints at the corners, and scarf or lap-joints between. The sills should be 2″ inside of the foundation-walls (see Fig. 1, Exercise 30). The **corner-posts,** b, are 4″ by 4″, and extend all the way to the roof. The **roof-plates,** d, are also 4″ by 4″, with half-joints at the corners, or, if the building has a gable-end, the joint may be like that in Fig. 2, Exercise 10. At c the corner-post is notched for the strip supporting the joists of the second story. This strip is 1″ by 5″. The **studs,** e, are 3″ by 4″, 13′ long, and set 16″ from centers; they are spliced as shown in Fig. 2, by nailing strips on the wide sides. The **floor-joists,** f, should be 3″ by 10″ for the principal floor, set against the studs, to which they are securely nailed. At g is the opening for the chimney; this opening is formed by mortising the **trimmer,** i, into the joists, h, h, 3′ from the studs; into this trimmer are mortised the joists, j. The form of mortising this case is that shown in Fig. 3, or the stronger joint formed by an iron strap, as in Fig. 4. To avoid waste, the openings for the windows may be calculated from the size of the glass; for a sash three lights wide and six high, each 8″ by 10″, the width will be 2′ 11″, and the height 6′. The studs for such openings are framed as at l and k. If a small building, the roof-joists may be 3″ by 6″, butting against the **ridge-pole,** m. If the upper story is an **attic,** its ceiling will be **hung,** supported, as at n, by light material. The floor-joists are stiffened by **bridging,** which is shown in Fig. 6. Two chalk-lines, as far apart as the joists are wide, are made across the tops of the joists where the bridging is to go, and from these lines the exact length and inclination of the saw-cut are obtained. Fig. 7 shows the manner of fastening beams or joists to brick walls, by using an **anchor.** Fig. 8 shows the manner of indicating the place for the foundation; the lines are fastened to nails driven into stakes. To **square** the lines with the tape-measure, lay off 8′ on one, and stick a pin through it at that point; on the other lay off 6′, and stick in a pin; the pins should be exactly 10′ apart to make the angle square.

Ex. 28.

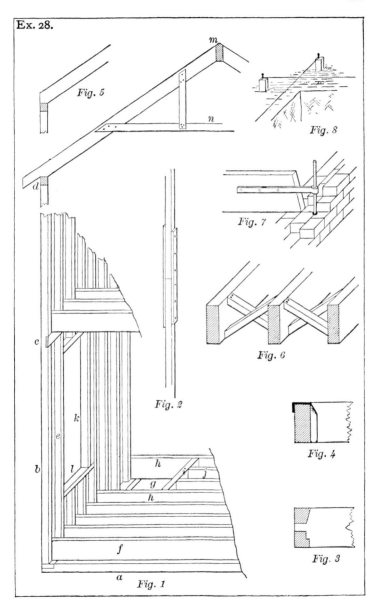

Fig. 5

m

n

Fig. 8

Fig. 7

Fig. 6

d

c

Fig. 2

k

e

b

l

h

g

j

h

Fig. 4

Fig. 3

f

a

Fig. 1

Exercise 29.—Construction of Window and Door Frames.

Material.—The following pieces enter into a window-frame the size of that mentioned in the previous Exercise:

Two *pulley-stiles,*	*a,* Figs. 1, 2, and 3,	$1\frac{1}{4}''$ thick,	$5''$	wide,	$6'\ 1''$ long.
One *head,*	*b,* Figs. 2 and 4,	$1\frac{1}{4}''$	"	$5''$	"	$2'\ 5\frac{3}{4}''$	"
One *sill,*	*c,* Figs. 1, 2, and 4,	$1\frac{1}{4}''$	"	$5\frac{1}{2}''$	"	$2'\ 5\frac{3}{4}''$	"
One *sub-sill,*	*d,* Figs. 1, 2, and 4,	$2''$	"	$6\frac{1}{4}''$	"	$3'\ 4''$	"
Two *casings,*	*e,* Figs. 1 and 2,	$\frac{7}{8}''$	"	$1\frac{3}{4}''$	"	$5'\ 6''$	"
One *casing,*	*f,* Figs. 1 and 2,	$\frac{7}{8}''$	"	$1\frac{3}{4}''$	"	$2'\ 7''$	"
Two *parting-strips,*	*g,* Figs. 1 and 2,	$\frac{1}{2}''$	"	$\frac{7}{8}''$	"	$5'\ 6''$	"
One *parting-strip,*	*h,* Fig. 2,	$\frac{1}{2}''$	"	$\frac{7}{8}''$	"	$2'\ 5\frac{3}{4}''$	"
Two *hanging-stiles,*	*i,* Fig. 1,	$1\frac{1}{4}''$	"	$4\frac{1}{2}''$	"	$5'\ 7''$	"
One *top,*	*j,* Fig. 1,	$1\frac{1}{4}''$	"	$4\frac{1}{2}''$	"	$3'\ 2''$	"

The pulley-stiles are grooved $1\frac{1}{2}''$ from the face-edge to receive the parting-strips, and at the top and bottom for the head and sills. The pulleys are let in with the chisel (*d,* Fig. 3); the **pocket** formed by two oblique saw-cuts, the bottom beveled with the chisel and secured by two small nails, and the top screwed (*e,* Fig. 3). The head *b,* sill *c,* and a portion of the sub-sill (*d,* Fig. 4), are of the same length, the sills beveled before nailing in place. The sub-sill should be grooved on the under side, to receive the siding, and prevent draughts under the window (*d,* Fig. 2).

The top parting-strip is the full length of the groove, the side parting-strips butting against it to hold it in place; usually none of these strips are nailed, the paint serving to secure them. If the hanging-stiles are chamfered, beaded, or molded, the joint with the top must be like that of Fig. 8, Exercise 16.

Door-frames are much simpler in construction. The diagrams, Figs. 5 and 6, give the necessary parts for an outside door $7'$ high and $2'\ 10''$ wide. The **jambs,** *a,* are rabbeted and grooved to receive the head. The sill is nailed to the ends of the jambs. Frames for inside doors are made of three pieces, the jambs and head.

Window and door-frames are built at the same time or before the frame is put up, and are placed in position before the siding is nailed on.

The diagrams in this Exercise are drawn to a scale of $\frac{1}{2}''$ to $1'$.

Ex. 29.

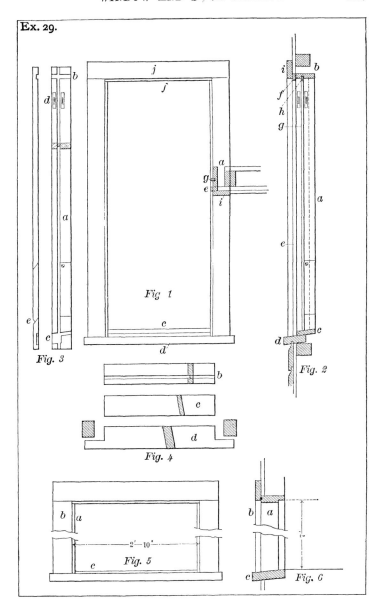

Fig 1

Fig. 3

Fig. 2

Fig. 4

Fig. 5

Fig. 6

Exercise 30.—Inclosing a Building.

A building is inclosed by sheathing, placing window and door frames in position, putting on building paper, siding and shingling.

If a frame is braced by oblique studs at the corners and possibly in the middle, the sheathing-boards are nailed on horizontally; but, if not braced by studs, it should be temporarily secured by oblique boards nailed on the inside of the studs, and the sheathing put on at about an angle of 45°. In Fig. 1, *a* represents the foundation, *b* the sill, *c*, *c* the studs, *e*, *e* the sheathing, which passes down over the sills, and is firmly nailed throughout.

Sheathing is usually composed of rough hemlock boards, 10″ wide, 1″ thick, and 13′ long.

The **water-table**, *g*, Fig. 1, is specially molded to cover the joint between the foundation and sills, and mitered at the corners. Next, the window and door frames are fastened in position, with the hanging-stiles against the sheathing, and the **corner-boards**, *i*, carefully nailed in place. These boards are usually $1\frac{1}{4}″$ thick, one 2″ wide and the other $3\frac{1}{4}″$ wide, and beaded, chamfered, or molded on the outer edge. The building paper is fastened to the sheathing with tacks, a little in advance of the siding (*f*, Fig. 1).

The siding is now put on, beginning at the bottom (*h*, *h*, Fig. 1). The joints between the boards are marked with try-square and pencil, and sawed very carefully to keep out wind and rain; the joints should always come opposite a stud for secure nailing. Two nails are driven at each stud, one in the middle of the board and the other just above the lap, as shown at *j*. Other forms of siding are shown at *k* and *l*, but are not as good as that at *h*.

Fig. 2 shows the preparation for shingles and the manner of putting them on. The first three layers (*c*, *d*, *e*) are put on overlapping, as shown at *b*; then, 6″ from the edge, a chalk-line is marked on the layer, *e*, and the next row, *f*, nailed with this line as a guide. The projecting part of the roof is finished with dressed boards, of which the one covering the ends of the rafters (*a*, Fig. 2) is put on last and should project about $\frac{1}{2}″$ below that covering the under sides.

Fig. 3 shows a form of gutter used on overhanging roofs, like that of Fig. 2. Fig. 4 shows the form of the usual tin-lined gutter.

In all work that is to be painted, the nails must be punched.

Ex. 30.

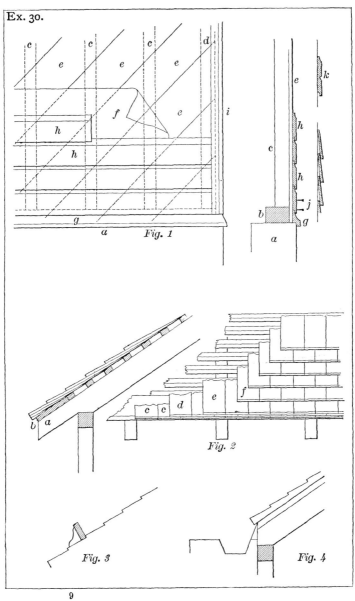

Fig. 1

Fig. 2

Fig. 3

Fig. 4

Exercise 31.—Laying Floors. Trimming.

Starting at one side, the floor-boards are laid with the tongued edge out (*a*, Fig. 1). Joints, *b*, marked with try-square and pencil, must come over a joist, and be as far removed from other joints as possible. Each board must be hammered up tight against the one behind it, using for this purpose a portion of a board with the groove, as shown at *c*. The nails are driven obliquely, near the face of the board on the tongued side, as shown at *d*, and with the drawn blow described in Exercise 4. If a joist is too low, a small chip must be placed between it and the floor-board before nailing; or if too high, it should be cut down with an adz. When the floor is complete, a smoothing-plane should be passed over those places where the boards are not flush.

Partitions are built by laying on the floor a stud, as at *e*, Fig. 1, and holding a corresponding one against the joists above; between these place the studs, 16″ from centers, using braces wherever possible. Studs are usually doubled at the doorways.

In trimming, the wood-work must be fitted to irregular plastered walls or floors by **scribing,** which is illustrated in Fig. 2. The **base-board,** *a*, is placed on blocks or nails a short distance above the floor, and the compasses, *c*, run along near its edge, so as to mark on it a line, *d*, corresponding to the uneven floor indicated by the broken line, *b*, *b*. The board is now sawed with a rip-saw, using the line *d* as a guide. By carefully adjusting the ends of the board to be scribed, the opposite edge may be brought flush with other portions of the trim.

Fig. 3 gives an example of a window-trim, with the shape indicated by shaded spaces. The base is returned at *a*. The inside sill, *d*, laps over the sill of the frame; *c* is the **stop-bead** which completes the groove in the frame for the lower sash; and the outer member of the molding, *b*, is scribed to the plastered wall.

Fig. 4 is an example of a simple wooden mantel. The bottom, *a*, is scribed to the floor, and the shelf, *b*, to the wall.

Fig. 5 gives a form of base. The board, *a*, is scribed to the floor, the molding, *b*, nailed to the studs, and the molding, *c*, nailed to the floor, thereby preventing draughts.

Ex. 31.

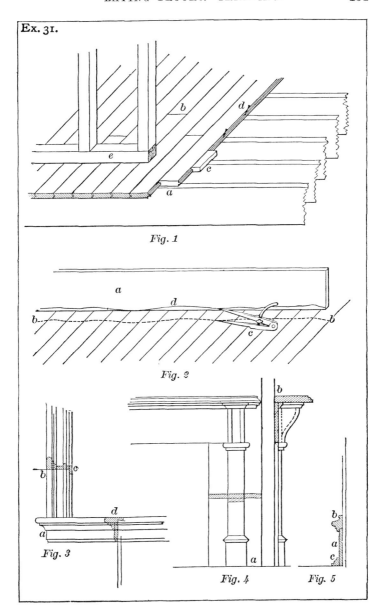

Fig. 1

Fig. 2

Fig. 3

Fig. 4

Fig. 5

Exercise 32.—Construction of a Sash.

While in former times the smaller size and greater cost of glass led to uniformity in the construction of the sash, at present there are few designers who think at all of adapting the window to the size of the glass; but, reversing that practice, design the window, and then cut the glass to fit.

The regular sizes for small panes are $6'' \times 8''$, $7'' \times 9''$, $8'' \times 10''$, $9'' \times 11''$, and $10'' \times 12''$, from which the sash and window-frame are easily computed, if the dimensions are laid off on **rods.** Fig. 1, a, shows one side of a rod, upon which is laid out the width of a sash to hold three $8''$ by $10''$ lights, and at b is shown the side of the rod on which is measured the height of the sash.

In Fig. 2 parts of the rod are enlarged to show the details of the marking, the letters corresponding with those of Fig. 1; c shows the **top-rail**, $2''$ wide, with a $1\frac{1}{4}''$ tenon. From the rabbet, which is $\frac{3}{16}$,$''$ for the glass in the top-rail, to that of the first **bar**, is $10\frac{1}{16}''$. The bar is $\frac{1}{2}''$ wide. At e is shown the **meeting-rail**, $1\frac{1}{4}''$, and at f the **bottom-rail.** From such a rod, carefully laid out, many sashes and frames may be marked out.

The rails and **stiles** are $1\frac{1}{2}''$ thick, and molded with a sash-plane; in the absence of which a flat chamfer will serve just as well.

The meeting-rails are made in one piece, as shown in Fig. 3: a is the upper stile with its mortise, b the lower stile, c the meeting-rail of the upper sash, and is not molded, but simply rabbeted for the glass; d, the meeting-rail for the lower sash, is molded, and not rabbeted; there is a groove about $\frac{1}{8}''$ wide and $\frac{3}{16}''$ deep for receiving the glass; the rails are sawed apart, as shown at e. When the sashes are put in the building, the bevels are planed and fitted tightly, as shown in Fig. 4.

The vertical bars are mortised through the rails, and have small mortises, $\frac{1}{2}''$ square, for the insertion of the horizontal bars, which are made the full width of the sash, but sawed into separate pieces just before putting together, as shown in Fig. 6.

Excepting those of the short bars, all of the joints are glued, the mortises wedged, and the dovetails pinned.

Fig. 5 shows the groove and socket for the **sash-cord**; a is plowed, and b bored with a long spoon-bit.

Ex. 32.

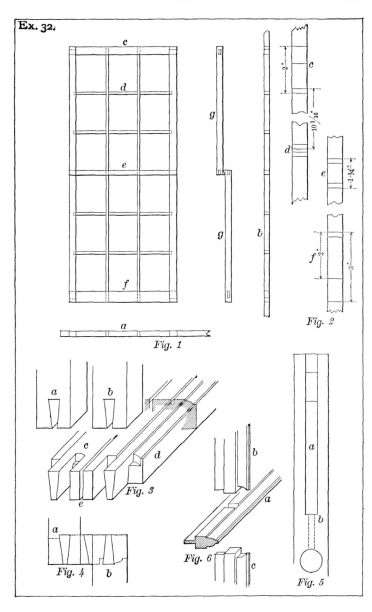

Fig. 1

Fig. 2

Fig. 3

Fig. 4

Fig. 5

Fig. 6

Exercise 33.—Construction of a Door.

Doors are either **batten** or **panel**.

Batten-doors are made by fastening several tongued and grooved boards to two or three cross-pieces, with clinch-nails or screws. If heavy, the doors should be braced with diagonal pieces between the cross-pieces.

The parts of a panel-door to fit the frame of Fig. 5, Example 29, are shown in Fig. 1 : *a* is the **top-rail**, *b* the **lock-rail**, *c* the **bottom-rail**, *d* the **stile**, *e* the **muntin**, and *f* a side view of the stile showing the mortises.

The joints are mortise and tenon, as indicated by the dotted lines. After the mortises and tenons are cut, the inner edges of the pieces are grooved to receive the panels.

Fig. 2 shows an enlarged view of the joint of the top-rail and stile : *a* is the tenon, $\frac{1}{2}''$ thick, *b* the **relish,** *c* the mortise, *e* the groove for the panel, and *d* the groove enlarged with a chisel to receive the relish. This may be taken as a sample for all of the joints. The tenon is at first the full width of the rail, and about $\frac{1}{4}''$ longer than the width of the stile.

The parts of the door, after the panels have been fitted, are glued, forced together by clamps such as that shown in Fig. 4, Exercise 19, and wedged.

The panels are plain, according to the section (Fig. 1), or raised, in which the material is thick, the sides cut down to fit the grooves, and the middle portion molded around its edge, as in Fig. 3, Exercise 39 ; or a plain panel molded, as in Fig. 6, Exercise 16.

Fig. 3 shows a portion of the frame of a blind or shutter ; it is made on the same principle as a door, but smaller ; the joints, instead of being glued and wedged, are white-leaded and pinned, and in place of panels may have **laths,** the ends of which have a projecting pin to fit into holes in the stiles of the frame. These holes must be bored to the same depth, and the distance between the ends of the pins of the lath should be a trifle greater than that between the bottoms of the holes in opposite stiles, or the laths will drop instead of retaining any position given them.

The **rod** is fastened to the laths with staples, one set of which is driven into the rod, and the other into the middle of the inner edge of the laths.

Ex. 33.

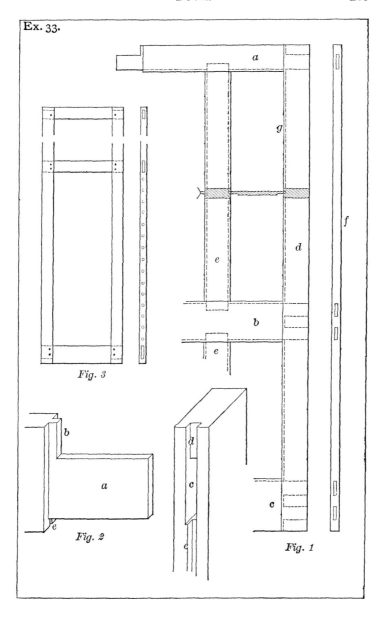

Fig. 3

Fig. 2

Fig. 1

Exercise 34.—Construction of Stairs.

For ordinary stairs, the single **step** should have a **riser** (a, Fig. 1), between $6\frac{1}{2}''$ and $7\frac{1}{2}''$ high, and a **tread,** b, from $9''$ to $11''$. The distance between the floors, say $9'\ 8''$, is measured in the building, and is divided to obtain a riser about the proper height, giving sixteen risers, $7\frac{1}{4}''$ high. If there are sixteen treads, and the space allowed for the stairs is $12'$, then it will require $9''$ for each.

After carefully measuring the space for the stairway, the height, width, and length, the work is laid out, cut, and partly put together in the workshop. From the height and length the **pitch,** or angle, of the stairs is determined.

The details for the step are shown in Fig. 1 : the riser, a, is $\frac{7}{8}''$ thick, grooved near the bottom of its face, and the outer end cut for a miter, as shown at d. The tread is $1\frac{3}{8}''$ or $1\frac{1}{2}''$ thick, tongued at b for insertion into the next riser, grooved on the under side near the front for its own riser, its front edge rounded, mitered at the end, and two dovetail mortises, c, c, to receive the balusters cut into the end, as shown at e. The tread and riser, with the quarter hollow molding, are glued together : sometimes to secure a better joint, blocks are glued in the angle under the tread, as shown in Fig. 4, Exercise 20.

Fig. 2 represents the **wall-string,** a, grooved to receive the steps, which are forced against the front edges, with wedges glued and driven at b, b, for both tread and riser. The bottom riser is not wedged.

Fig. 3 shows the **face-string,** the upright edges of which are mitered as at b ; the edge, c, is square, to receive the treads, which are firmly nailed near the base of the baluster. The face-string is usually stiffened by a stud or joist, as at e, Fig. 3.

A plain **newel** is shown in Fig. 4. The section at a shows the structure through the base and the way in which it is fastened to the riser, b, and the string, c, the tread being cut away to allow it to pass down to the floor.

Fig. 5 shows the balusters; the shorter, a, coincides with the face of the riser, the longer, b, is placed with its face one half way between the risers.

After the balusters are in position, the molding is completed on the face-string, as in the upper part of Fig. 4.

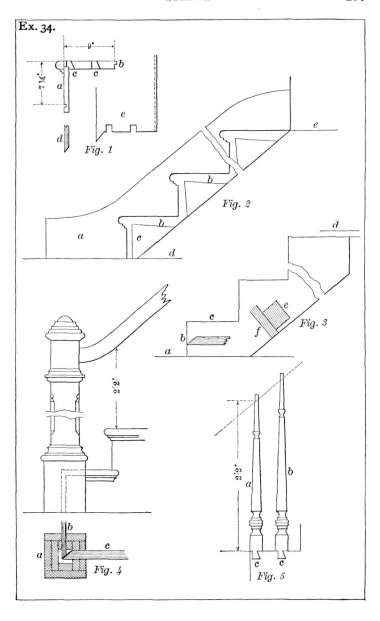

Ex. 34.

Fig. 1

Fig. 2

Fig. 3

Fig. 4

Fig. 5

Exercise 35.—Laying out and shaping the Hand-rail.

The **hand-rail** should always have a gradual and graceful change from one direction to another. In Fig. 1, *a b* represents a tread, *b d* a riser, and *a d* the pitch, which is the direction of the hand-rail; *c* a point on the axis of the cylinder around which the stairs turn; *a e* a quarter of an ellipse, and represents the bending of the center of the hand-rail in passing from the inclined to the horizontal position; *e g* a quadrant, through which the center of the hand-rail bends before becoming straight again.

This double bending, or **wreath,** is made in two pieces, joined at *e*. We will take for illustration the elliptical one. In Fig. 2, *c* represents the axis of the cylinder at the **landing,** *d* the face of the string, *e* the line of the balusters and center of the hand-rail, *a c* the tread, *a b* the riser, *c b* the pitch, *a b c* the angle used in marking the work; *c g* and *g i* are semi-diameters of the ellipse through which the hand-rail passes.

With the lengths *c g* and *g i*, of Fig. 2, construct the lines *a b* and *b c* of Fig. 3; with *i h*, of Fig. 2, lay off *a f* and *a h* in Fig. 3; with *g f*, of Fig. 2, lay off *c e* and *c d* in Fig. 3, and complete the elliptical form, *f e d h*. This form, the **mold,** is cut out of a thin board, and used in laying out the work.

Fig. 4 represents a block of wood, thicker than the hand-rail, and sawed to the form of the mold. With a T-bevel adjusted to the angle, *a b c*, of Fig. 2, and applied to the side, *d e*, Fig. 3, slide the mold along the line *a b*, Fig. 3, until the center of the hand-rail in this inclined position comes to the center of the end of the wood, as shown at *e g*, Fig. 3. A rectangle, inclosing the form of the rail, is now drawn on the end, *e g*, and also on the end at *j*, Fig. 3. The corners of these rectangles are now united by curved lines drawn along a thin straight-edge pressed to the hollow and round surfaces, as in Fig. 4.

The block is then cut to these lines, producing a shape as shown in Fig. 5—in which it must be remembered the side *a*, and also that directly opposite, are cylindrical surfaces.

The elements of the molding are now marked from the edges, and worked with gouge, spoke-shave, and planes specially shaped for the purpose. In practice a straight portion of the rail is worked on the same block with the wreath, *a h* and *g h'*, Fig. 1.

Ex. 35.

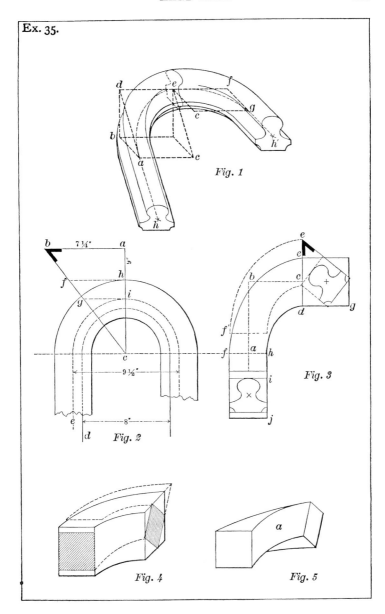

Fig. 1

Fig. 2

Fig. 3

Fig. 4

Fig. 5

Exercise 36.—Use of the Frame-Saw. Bending Wood.

For small work, a narrow saw, with fine teeth, as at *a, b*, Fig. 1, is used ; but for ordinary carpenter's **scroll-work,** a saw like that shown at *c* and *d*, held in a frame, as in Fig 4, Plate B, is employed. The back of the saw is beveled to turn easily when cutting small circles, and it will cut better if drawn very tight.

To cut out a circular hole in a board, bore first with a center-bit (*a*, Fig. 2), close up to the line, then start the saw from this hole, as at *b*. In cutting narrow angles in scroll-work, the saw is sent all the way into the corner, as at *a*, Fig. 3, then backed·up to cut as shown at *b*, the piece *c* is taken out, the saw turned and the piece cut, as at *d*. Scroll-work is finished with the chisel, spokeshave, or rasp, and smoothed with sand-paper.

There are many ways of bending wood, but the best is to steam and bend it around a form, as shown in Fig. 4. The form, *a*, is fastened to a plank or the shop-floor, the piece, *b*, steamed thoroughly, bent in place, and held until dry by blocks nailed against it, as at *d ;* or, if several pieces are to receive the same shape, by pins driven into holes, as at *c*. Boat-builders use planks with pins on both sides of the steamed stick in bending the ribs. Pieces to be bent with steam are usually worked to the desired shape first, then bent, and when dry are finished with the spoke-shave.

In bending moldings, if steam is not convenient, they may be sawed, as shown at *a*, Fig. 5 and Fig. 6. In bending the face-string of stairs, the method shown in Fig. 7 is employed. The string has a series of grooves cut parallel with the axis of the cylinder around which the string is to bend ; it is then wet with hot water, and bent over a cylinder, or **saddle,** and the strips, *a*, fitted and glued in. When the glue has set, the tops of the strips may be planed down, and a piece of canvas glued over the bent portion. Fig. 8 shows another method of arriving at the same result, in which the string acts as a sort of veneer to the pieces, *a*. Where a bend and twist are to be given, the wood may be made up of several thin pieces glued together, as in Fig. 9.

In bending wood, compress the fibers on the inside of the curve, to retain its strength.

The curve of the form (*a*, Fig. 4) should be a little quicker, to allow for a slight spring back of the wood when released.

Ex. 36.

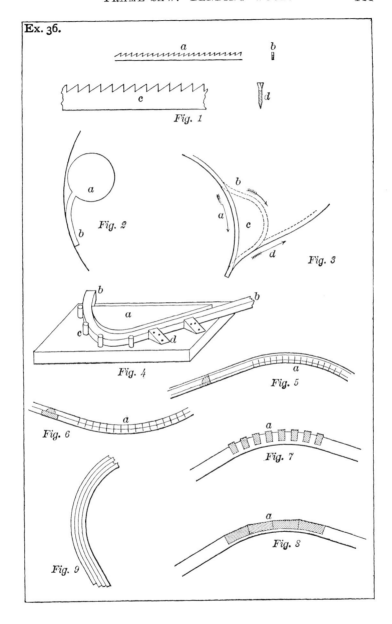

Fig. 1

Fig. 2

Fig. 3

Fig. 4

Fig. 5

Fig. 6

Fig. 7

Fig. 8

Fig. 9

Exercise 37.—Construction of a Pattern.

Pattern makers receive drawings of finished iron-work; from these drawings they must lay out and construct the wood-work necessary to obtain molds for the castings.

Fig. 1 represents a cast-iron **pillow-block,** to receive an inch-shaft; Fig. 2, the plan of the **box** without the **cap.** The surfaces through, from *a* to *b*, Fig. 1, are to be **finished.**

Fig. 3 represents the pattern for the cap; it is made of four pieces, *a, b, c, d*, nailed together.

The measures taken from the drawings, or specifications, are increased a small amount, about $\frac{1}{8}''$ to $1'$, to allow for shrinkage of the iron.

Those surfaces which are to be finished should be about $\frac{1}{16}''$ thicker than shown in the drawings. In Fig. 3 the wood beyond the broken line, *e, e*, shows the allowance made on the pattern for finishing.

The smoothest surface, containing the least number of **blow-holes,** on a casting, is the one which was down; therefore, the pattern must be built with that in view. In order to facilitate drawing the pattern from the sand, it should have its vertical sides slightly inclined and very smooth.

The base, Fig. 4, is made of the several pieces, *a, b, c, d*, and *e*, to secure smoother surfaces than could be obtained by cutting the pattern from a solid block. The lower part of the piece, *d*, may be made separately.

The holes for the bolts are either to be bored in the metal or **cored.** In the latter case, a **core-print,** *f*, is fastened in the proper place, and the molder inserts in the mold a core of the proper size.

The box is to have hollows, to receive Babbit metal linings; these hollows must be cored out; *c*, Fig. 3, and *e*, Fig. 4, are the core-prints, and Fig. 6, the core-box for the hollows, which are indicated by broken lines in Figs. 3, 4, and 5. The core-box is made of five pieces; the block, *a*, with the thin pieces, *b*, nailed to its ends; the pieces, *c, c*, held in position by dowels, are removed, to free the core.

The pattern has its nail-holes filled with wax or putty, and is varnished with shellac dissolved in alcohol. The core-prints are covered with shellac varnish in which lamp-black has been mixed.

Ex. 37.

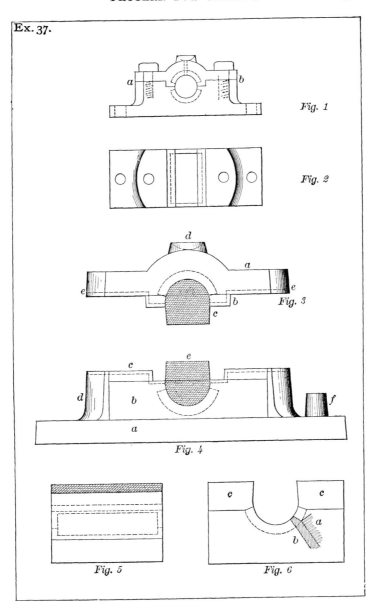

Fig. 1

Fig. 2

Fig. 3

Fig. 4

Fig. 5

Fig. 6

Exercise 38.—Shaping a Boat-Model.

Material.—A block of pine, 2″ high, 1¾″ wide, and 9″ long.

Work.—To chisel out a half-model, conforming to the lines given in the plans.

The design, which is that of a common yawl, is divided into spaces, 1″ apart, as shown in Fig. 1 and Fig. 2; $a b$ represents the water-line, and $c d$ an arbitrary vertical section through the model.

Fig. 3 gives the full size and form of the model for each inch. The numbers correspond with those of Figs. 1 and 2.

With tracing-paper transfer these curves to cardboard or thin veneers; cut the hollow sides, thus forming **templates,** which are to be used in testing the work as it progresses.

Mark all around the block pencil-lines 1″ apart. Lay off on these lines the vertical heights of each of the spaces on the front and back of the block, and through the points thus obtained draw curves representing the deck. Chisel down the top to these lines, and restore the inch lines on the deck surface.

Lay off on the inch lines of the deck the horizontal widths of each, and, drawing a curve through these, obtain the outer curve of Fig. 2. On the bottom lay off the widths to obtain the inner curve, e, Fig. 2. Saw the inclinations of bow and stern, and mark on the stern end the shape of that part from its template. In order to hold the block its flat side may be fastened with screws to another block and the curved side shaped with the chisel and gouge. When finished, the model may be fastened to a thin hardwood piece, as shown in Figs. 1 and 2, making it more ornamental; or, for a better effect, the block may be built up of ½″ pieces and thin dark veneers, all glued or screwed together.

Besides testing with the templates, the fingers should be passed lightly over the side, to detect high and irregular places, which must be pared down.

Finish with fine sand-paper held in the fingers.

In practice the boat-builder constructs his models of thin pieces, usually ½″ thick, dowelled together, so that they may be easily taken apart. After shaping the model the pieces are marked, separated, and the measures obtained from the pieces give him the details with which he makes the curves on the block (Fig. 4, Exercise 36) for bending the ribs.

Ex. 38.

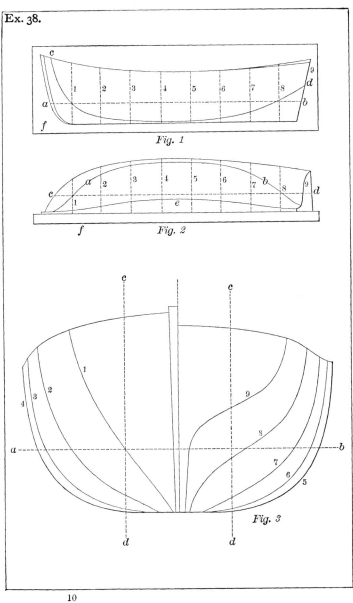

Fig. 1

Fig. 2

Fig. 3

Exercise 39.—Veneering.

Material.—Block of pine large enough to furnish a cube of 3″.

Six pieces of veneers, preferably of different woods and as near the same thickness as possible.

Work.—1. To plane the cube.

2. Glue veneers on opposite surfaces.

3. Polish the veneers.

One of the most effective ways of finishing wood is to cover it with a thin layer of some fancy variety. Sometimes the fancy wood lacks strength, or can not be obtained sufficiently large, or possibly is too expensive to be used in solid form. Then, to obtain its effect, a common wood must be used as a base and the fancy wood as a veneer.

Veneers are of varying thickness, from $\frac{1}{32}$″ up to $\frac{1}{4}$″. Because of the greater tendency of hard wood to warp and shrink, structures like doors are made with an inside of pine and outer coats of veneers, $\frac{1}{4}$″ or more in thickness. For ordinary cabinet-work, veneers are about $\frac{1}{16}$″ thick.

Thick veneers, as *a*, in Fig. 1, are prepared for gluing, as directed in Exercise 19. The surface should always be scratched, unless the wood holds glue very well.

The cube, Fig. 2, is made true by carefully sawing and planing the ends first, and from them squaring the sides. The ends and sides must be perfectly flat, or the veneers will receive no support at the corners.

The ends are now **sized**—that is, coated with very thin glue, to cause better adhesion.

The veneers, *g*, Fig. 2, are cut at least $\frac{1}{8}$″ larger all around than the size of the block, roughened with the iron of the scratch-plane, taken out of the plane, and held in the hand; and the opposite side marked with a pencil to distinguish the surface.

Next, prepare two **cauls** (*h*, Fig. 2), $\frac{1}{2}$″ larger all around than a face of the cube, about 1″ thick, and with one side very flat. These are kept hot when ready for use.

Cover the scratched surface of two veneers and the ends of the cube with glue; place the veneers on the ends, the hot cauls on the veneers, and apply the hand-screws with great care. The hot cauls remelt the glue, and therefore this operation need not be hastened

Ex. 39.

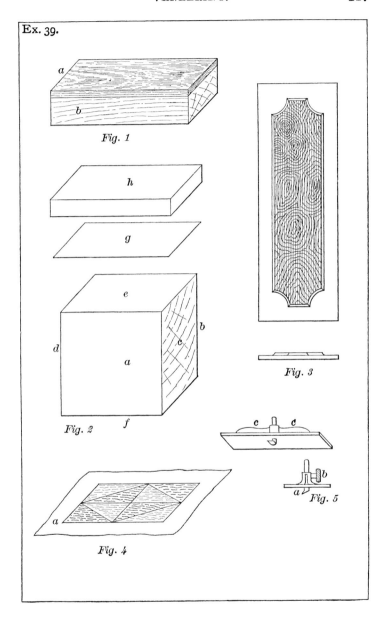

Fig. 1

Fig. 2

Fig. 3

Fig. 4

Fig. 5

as in the case of ordinary gluing. If the veneers are split or have small holes through which the glue may ooze, place a piece of thick paper between the cauls and veneers to prevent them from adhering.

When thoroughly dry, the veneers are trimmed, and the next pair glued on.

The veneered surfaces are now planed with a block-plane or very true smoothing-plane, observing the directions in Exercise 24, then sand-papered, coated with a filling varnish, and set aside to harden.

If it is desired to put fancy designs in veneers on the cube, they should first be sawed, and if straight, edged with the plane, in the position shown in Fig. 7, Exercise 15, and glued to a piece of strong paper, as in Fig. 4. This is then scratched and glued on in place of the single piece.

The raised portion of panels is frequently veneered, as shown in Fig. 3. In this case the veneer should be of the same kind of wood, as a walnut-root veneer on a walnut panel. Strong contrasts should be avoided.

In cabinet-work, recesses are sometimes cut to receive veneers; these may be cut out with the chisel, or, better, with a **router,** shown in Fig. 5; *a* is the cutting-edge, projecting the proper depth below the smooth surface of the tool, adjusted and fastened by the pinch-screw, *b; c, c,* are projections against which the thumbs are applied in pushing the tool.

Wooden routers may be made of a thick piece of hard wood, with a throat for the insertion of a chisel and wedge to secure it.

A very small veneer may be set by gluing and holding a hot iron against it for a few moments. This is of service in repairing broken or loose veneers.

Bags of hot sand are sometimes used as cauls in veneering uneven surfaces.

Polishing.

Fasten the veneered cube in the vise, using cloth between the jaws and the cube. If it is too low, a hand-screw may be fastened in the vise and the cube held in the hand-screw. The work will be hastened if the pores of open-grained woods are closed with a filler. This filler, which may be obtained already prepared, or made by mixing chalk or plaster with turpentine to a paste, is rubbed in with a cotton cloth, and the cube set aside for a few hours to become nearly dry, when the excess of the filler is removed with a sharp steel scraper, and the surface smoothed with fine sand-paper moved in the direction of the grain.

To polish, take a wad of cotton as large as a walnut, place it within a clean cotton cloth about 5″ square, and saturate with shellac varnish; twist the corners of the cloth, hold in the fingers, and pass a finger moistened with a drop of raw linseed-oil over the surface of the **rubber.** Apply the rubber with small circular strokes until the entire surface has been gone over, and the grain seems filled. Turn the cube and go over the same process with each of the other sides. Set the cube aside for a day. Repeat the process, scraping and sand-papering, if necessary, and again rubbing in varnish with a new rubber until the sunken spots are filled. If the rubber begins to stick, it must be slightly oiled, but the least amount of oil used the better for the polishing. To finish, moisten a clean cloth with a few drops of alcohol, and rub the surface briskly for a minute or two. The palm of the hand is frequently used to put the finishing touch to a polished surface; this should be done before the varnish becomes hard.

If furniture varnish is used, the wood is filled, then covered with several coats of varnish, applied with a flat brush, allowing each coat to become perfectly hard, and smoothing with fine sand-paper before the next is put on; the surface is then polished with rotten-stone and petroleum, and rubbed perfectly dry with cloths or cotton-waste.

Painting.

A new brush should stand in linseed-oil ten or twelve hours, after which it is ready for use. When finished the brush should be thoroughly cleaned with turpentine, and put aside in such a way that the bristles are not bent, but lie out straight. The bristles may be wrapped in cloth or paper to prevent them from spreading. In the absence of turpentine, kerosene or soap and water will clean the brush nearly as well.

To prepare work for painting, the nails should be **punched**— that is, driven about $\frac{1}{16}$″ below the surface, and the wood sand-papered. In sand-papering a soft wood, coarse paper is bent around a block, 3″ by 5″ and 1″ thick, with a layer of cork, ¼″ thick, glued to its face; the wood is gone over with oblique and circular strokes to cut down ridges and high places, then a few strokes with the grain to remove scratches. Next, with a fine paper and the block rub only in the direction of the grain until very smooth. Surfaces to be varnished or polished should always be sand-papered with the grain. Before painting pine-woods, the knots and resin-pockets must be covered with size, or, better, with thick shellac-varnish.

The first, or **priming** coat, is a mixture of white-lead, raw and boiled linseed-oils; or, it may contain red-lead and other pigments and turpentine; but, in any case, the drying-oil is in greater and the pigment in less proportion than in ordinary paint. To obtain an even flow of paint from the brush, hold it nearly perpendicular to the surface, and allow the ends only of the bristles to touch.

When the priming is dry, the nail-holes, cracks, and defects generally are puttied, and the work smoothed with sand-paper, if small.

The work is then painted two or more coats with the regular mixture of white-lead, oil, and turpentine, lightly sand-papering the first and second, if very smooth work is desired. The strokes should be long, even, and with the grain. If the subject is a door, paint the panels first, then the muntins, next the rails, and lastly the styles, thus making the brush-marks correspond to the grain of the wood.

For inside work the paint should contain about one half as much turpentine as oil, which, in drying, will give a dull surface; but for outside work little or no turpentine should be used to secure a good and lasting surface, and, in drying, the surface retains its luster.

INDEX.

Grain, fine, 25.
   silver, 25.
   straight, 24.
Grindstone, 82.
Grooved joints, 88.
Growth of trees, 19.
   spring, 14, 16.
   summer, 14, 16.
Grub, beetle, 46.
Gunstock, 34.
Gutter, 128.

Half-joint, 86.
   modified forms of, 88.
Hammer, 57, 70.
Hand-rail, 104, 138.
Hand-screw, 58, 106.
Hanging-stile, 126.
Hardness, 18, 25, 38.
Head of frame, 126.
Heart-wood, 14, 18.
Hemlock, 28, 30, 38.
Hickory, 19, 26, 34, 38.
Hinge, 118.
Hollow-plane, 60.
Hook and eye, 118.
Hooked teeth of saw, 76.
Horn-bug, 50.
Hung ceiling, 124.
Hymenomycetes, 43.

Immersion of wood in water, 21, 27, 52.
   of logs in water, 52.
Inclosing a building, 128.
Insects, parasitic, 19, 45.
Iron, plane, 60.

Jack-plane, 60, 72.
Jambs of door, 126.
Jaws of beetle, 47.
Jersey pine, 30.
Joinery, 40.
Joint, blind-dovetail, 122.
   blind-mortise, 94.
   bolted, 94.

Joint, dovetail, 69.
   dowel, 104.
   glued, 106, 114.
   grooved, 88.
   half, 86, 88.
   keyed, 86.
   lap, 88.
   miter, 98, 102.
   mortise, 90.
   oblique-dovetail, 88.
   of studs, 124.
   pinned, 92.
   rabbeted, 88.
   scarf, 86.
   screwed, 108.
   shoulder of, 88.
   stretcher, 102.
   stub-mortise, 94.
   water-tight, 88.
   wedged, 86.
Jointer, 60.

Kerf, 76.
Kiln-dried wood, 22.
Kinds of wood, 30.
Knarls, 51.
Knife, bench, 58.
   marking with, 78.
Knots, 28.

Ladder-form vessels, 17.
Lap-joint, 88.
Larva, 46.
Lath, blind, 134.
Laying floors, 130.
Laying out material, 110.
Level, spirit, 58.
Lignin, 18.
Lignum-vitæ, 36, 38.
   sap-wood of, 52.
Lips of beetle, 47.
Lock-rail, 134.
Locust 35, 38, 53.
Logs immersed in water, 21, 27, 52.
   prepared for shipping, 52.

Parasitic insects, 45.
    plants, 41.
Paring, 64.
Parting-strips, 126.
Partitions, 130.
Patterns for casting, 30, 36, 142.
Pearwood, 35.
Pencil, 58.
Perspective, 62.
Picture-frames, 102.
Pillow-block, 142.
Pine group, 13, 15, 16, 30.
    Jersey, 30.
    white, 19, 27, 30, 38.
    yellow, 30, 38.
    weevil, 49.
Pinning a mortise, 92,
Pitch of stairs, 136.
Pith, 13, 14, 15, 32.
Pits, bordered, 15, 16.
Pitted vessels, 14, 17.
Plane, 72, 74.
    block, 116.
    fore, 60.
    hollow, 60.
    jack, 60, 72.
    jointing, 60.
    match, 60.
    rabbet, 60.
    round, 60.
    sash, 60, 132.
    scratch, 60, 106, 146.
    smoothing, 60, 74, 116.
Plane-iron, 60, 72, 80, 82.
Plane-stock, 60.
Plank, 22.
Plants, parasitic, 41.
Plow, 60, 120.
Plumb-bob, 58.
Pocket in window-frame, 126.
    resin, 28, 150.
Polishing, 148.
Polypore, 41, 43.
Polyporus annosus, 43.
    dryadeus, 44.

Polyporus, fulvus, 44.
    pini, 44.
    sulphurus, 43.
Porosity, 25.
Preservation of wood, 52.
Priming-coat, 150.
Prionus unicolor, 50.
Properties of wood, 24.
Pulley-stile, 126.
Pupa, 46.

Quirk, 68.

Rabbet, 88.
Rabbet-plane, 60.
Rail, bottom, 132, 134.
    lock, 134.
    meeting, 132.
    top, 132, 134.
Raked teeth of saw, 76.
Rattan, 26, 32.
Reamer, 60.
Red cedar, 19, 31, 38.
    oak, 33, 38.
Redwood, 19, 31, 38, 53.
Relish, 134.
Resawing lumber, 22, 23.
Resin, 16, 25, 27.
    pockets, 28, 150.
Return molding, 68.
Ridge-pole, 124.
Right angle, 58.
Ringed vessels, 17.
Rip-saw, 76.
    filing, 84.
    use of the, 76, 102.
Riser, 136.
Rod for marking, 132.
    blind, 134.
Roebuck beetle, 50.
Roof-plate, 124.
Rosewood, 37.
Rot of wood, 42.
Round-plane, 60.
Router, 148.

THE END.

APPLETONS'
STANDARD GEOGRAPHIES.

Comprehensive, Attractive, Up to Date.

THE SERIES:

Appletons' Elementary Geography.

This book treats the subject objectively, makes knowledge precede definitions, and presents facts in their logical connections, taking gradual steps from the known to the unknown. The work is designed to be **elementary**, not only in name and size, but also in the style and quality of its matter and development of the subject. The illustrations have been selected with great care, and the maps are distinct, unencumbered with names, accurate, and attractive.

Introduction price, 55 cents.

Appletons' Higher Geography.

This volume is not a repetition of the Elementary, either in its matter or mode of developing the subject. In it the earth is viewed as a whole, and the great facts of political as depending on the physical geography are fully explained. Great prominence is given to commerce and leading industries as the result of physical conditions. The maps challenge comparison in point of correctness, distinctness, and artistic finish. Special State editions, with large, beautiful maps and descriptive matter, supplied without additional expense.

Introduction price, $1.25.

Appletons' Physical Geography.

The new Physical Geography stands unrivaled among text-books on the subject. Its list of authors includes such eminent scientific specialists as Quackenbos, Newberry, Hitchcock, Stevens, Gannett, Dall, Merriam, Britton, Lieutenant Stoney, George F. Kunz, and others, presenting an array of talent never before united in the making of a single text-book.

Introduction price, $1.60.

Specimen copies, for examination, will be sent, post-paid, to teachers and school-officers, on receipt of the introduction prices.

Liberal terms made to schools for introduction and exchange.

AMERICAN BOOK COMPANY, Publishers,

NEW YORK,   ·:·   CINCINNATI,   ·:·   CHICAGO.